If you've ever stood in your closet in tears because you simply had no clue what to wear, this is the book for you. If you've ever headed off to the store only to be completely overwhelmed, this is the book for you. If you're tired of feeling frumpy, dumpy, and out of style, this is the book for you. All these things used to be true for me before I applied the truths found in Shari's book. She will help you look great by maximizing your good features and minimizing your less-than-favorite ones, and you'll save money by only buying clothes you'll feel confidently fantastic wearing. Every woman should have this invaluable resource!

> **Lysa TerKeurst,** speaker and *New York Times* bestselling author of *Becoming More Than a Good Bible Study Girl*, *Made to Crave*, and *Unglued*

Can faith and fashion go together? You bet, especially if you're Shari Braendel, whose own faith is evident throughout. No matter your age, shape, or style, she offers great tips and practical advice to help you look your best and be your best, inside and out.

> **Ann Spangler,** author of *Women of the Bible*

Every women longs for a makeover of some kind and Shari Braendel offers just that ... in book form! This book offers women the information they desperately desire. Her fashion wisdom blended with God's truth and perspective helps women to be good stewards of the body God has given them. Shari helps women dress the body shape they have in an affordable, everyone-can-do-this kind of way!

> **Jill Savage,** founder of Hearts at Home and author of *Living With Less So Your Family Has More* and *No More Perfect Moms*

Good Girls Don't Have to Dress Bad threw a life ring to this non-girly-girl who battles fashion bewilderment. Part helpful beauty manual, part Jesus-loves-you pep talk, this book will help women embrace their bodies and their Lord — with panache and confidence.

> **Mary DeMuth,** author of *Thin Places: A Memoir, Beautiful Battle,* and *Everything*

❧

Shari's message is so engaging and fun and yet it is so important. Nearly every woman subconsciously wonders, *am I beautiful?* and wants to look and feel her best — and this great book is just what we need to get there. The last time I was with Shari I kept seeking her advice about clothes, styles, and colors — all of which has proven invaluable to me. And now, in this book, you can have the same!

> **Shaunti Feldhahn,** best-selling author of *For Women Only*

❧

I carry a bigger bag when I shop just so I can carry *Help Me Jesus! I Have Nothing to Wear!* I don't leave home without it. Not only does Shari's fashion advice give me more confidence when I get dressed each morning, it gives me more confidence where a woman needs it most — in the dressing room.

Change your clothes, change your life. Buy this book.

> **Kathi Lipp,** Author of *The Get Yourself Organized Project* and *The Husband Project*

HELP ME, JESUS!

I have nothing to wear!

HELP ME, JESUS!
I have nothing to wear!

Previously published as *GOOD GIRLS DON'T HAVE TO DRESS BAD*

THE GO-TO GUIDE FOR ALL SHAPES AND SIZES

SHARI BRAENDEL

ZONDERVAN®

ZONDERVAN

Help Me, Jesus! I Have Nothing to Wear!
Formerly *Good Girls Don't Have to Dress Bad*
Copyright © 2010 by Shari Braendel

This title is also available as a Zondervan ebook.
Visit www.zondervan.com/ebooks.

Requests for information should be addressed to:

Zondervan, 3900 *Sparks Drive SE, Grand Rapids, Michigan 49546*

This edition: ISBN 978-0-310-33975-5 (softcover)

Library of Congress Cataloging-in-Publication Data

Braendel, Shari, 1961–
        Good girls don't have to dress bad : a style guide for every woman / Shari Braendel.
            p.   cm.
        ISBN 978-0-310-32601-4 (softcover)
        1. Christian women—Religious life. 2. Beauty, Personal—Religious aspects—
Christianity. 3. Women's clothing. 4. Fashion. I. Title.
        BV4527.B6814   2009
        248.8'43.43—dc22   2009046387

Published in association with the literary agency of Fedd & Company, Inc., 9759 Concord Pass, Brentwood, TN 37027.

Cover photography: Laurence Monneret / Getty Images®
Interior design: Beth Shagene
Interior illustration: Monika Roe
Interior photography: See page 199

Printed in China

14 15 16 17 18 19 20 /DSC/ 23 22 21 20 19 18 17 16 15 14 13 12 11 10 9 8 7 6 5 4 3 2 1

To the outstanding Christian Image Consultants
who have completed my CIC training program.
You make the world a more beautiful place.

To Donna, sister of the heart and BFF,
thank you for coming up with the title of this book
and for always checking behind me
to make sure I haven't forgotten anything.
I'm certain old age will find us walking in airports together
dressed in pink with big hair!

And to Lucy,
I know that Jesus waits to hear from you each morning.
Thank you from the bottom of my heart
for taking my prayer requests
before Him each and every day.

To each of you;
my ministry is your ministry.

Contents

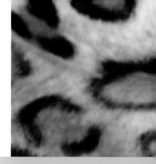

What's So Christian about Looking Good?

LOOKS **DO** MATTER.

There. I said it. Now hang with me here.

If you are a Christian, then your faith plays a part in every aspect of your life. Or at least it should. Faith affects your personal life, your career choices, and your family relationships (whether you are married, single, or divorced). Faith affects your music and movie selections and where you hang out or what you do for fun.

Your faith even colors your clothing choices. Now don't start groaning on me. You have a responsibility as a Christian female to make sure that how you dress is a reflection of who you really are. I'm not suggesting you walk around wearing "I Love Jesus" T-shirts and wristbands, but you have to live knowing that what you put on in the morning says something about your character.

Christian circles, especially churches, rarely discuss outer appearance. None of us wants anyone else to think we might be vain or conceited because we focus, on some level, on what we look like. We're holy and modest Christians, after all. Our lives are all about inner beauty, right? Not entirely. Stay with me for a little bit. I'm going to circle right back to inner beauty in a few.

Guess what, girlfriend? The truth is, most of us are watching any reality TV to get a clue on how to dress right and look good. We hungrily purchase fashion magazines any time the cover article has something to do with how we can hide our despised body parts. We make mad dashes to the local department store to pick up the new anti-wrinkle cream Dr. Oz promised us will take ten years away from our face.

The bottom line? We do care about our looks. Why is that? Because we're women and women love to look and feel good. God made us that way. He made me that way. He made you that way. And this is not a bad thing. In fact, it's a wonderful thing.

Do you notice that the woman mentioned in Proverbs 31 is clothed in fine linen and purple, strength and dignity (vv. 22, 25)? It doesn't say she puts on her ratty sweatpants and old T-shirt to go about her business. She takes some time with herself. If God addresses a woman's outside appearance in the Bible (and He didn't have to do that), He must think it's important for us to talk about too. In the same vein, God also refers to this woman's insides when He mentions her strength and dignity. If you go back a few verses (v. 15) you'll notice she gets up at the crack of dawn, and I wouldn't be surprised if she starts her day by being with the Lord.

In the back of your mind, you're probably thinking about the apostle Peter's advice to Christian wives: "Your beauty should not come from outward adornment, such as braided hair and the wearing of gold jewelry and fine clothes. Instead, it should be that of your inner self, the unfading beauty of a gentle and quiet spirit, which is of great worth in God's sight. For this is the way the holy women of the past who put their hope in God used to make themselves beautiful" (1 Peter 3:3 – 5).

The NIV Study Bible explains that "outward adornment" has to do with "extreme coiffures and gaudy exhibits of jewelry and expensive garments."[1] If our idea of beauty is based on what we put on, rather than our relationship with the Creator of beauty, we've got a problem. In other words, if you're messed up on the inside, three gold bracelets probably aren't going to make it all better. You might just want to go spend fifteen minutes alone with God to start working on your inside stuff. When we feel precious, redeemed, and loved by our Savior, we won't have a need to impress with ostentatious clothing, jewelry, or handbags. Instead, we'll find an appropriate way to dress to reflect what's going on inside of us.

If our idea of beauty is based on what we put on, rather than our relationship with the Creator of beauty, we've got a problem.

Introduction:

A few summers ago I walked into a department store and saw the purse of all purses. Oh, let me tell you, this bag was the mack daddy of bags! It was the biggest, grandest, most beautiful Coach bag I had ever seen. I asked the sales associate to unlock it from its case. This bag was so expensive and grandiose it needed to be put behind glass walls! The sales associate mentioned that she was told in a Coach training school that if you were ever lost in the desert, this bag would certainly be all one would need. I was very impressed (tickled pink, really) and asked her the question I was avoiding.

"How much is it?" I squeaked.

She told me the price just as my husband, who has a gift for great timing, approached the counter. He kindly told the woman no thank you and started to pull me away. Yes, pull, as in drag my body away from the store with my heels digging into the floor.

"Can you hold the bag for me?" I yelled back. Of course she could.

For weeks all I could think about was that purse. I would go to sleep and wake up thinking about how amazing this purse would look with my outfits. I even dreamed about it one night.

One morning I was having my quiet time, and as I was praying I heard God whisper to my heart. He said, "I don't care if they GIVE you that purse, you can't have it." Excuse me, God, but did you just tell me I can't have that purse? That beautiful, amazing, mack daddy purse I might need if I'm ever stuck in the desert? Yup, He sure did.

The truth was, I didn't see how a purse could be such a big deal for God, but the more I prayed, the more I understood. My thoughts had become consumed by that purse. I had been spending more time obsessing about a simple accessory than I had obsessing about God.

I tell you this story because I want you to know that it's NOT all about what we wear or don't wear. If your heart's not right, if your relationship with God is suffering, then no matter what we put on, we aren't that beautiful.

Friend, our inside *and* our outside matters. God says so. It's time to learn how to care for our outside appearance, not in an ostentatious kind of way, but in a sensible, easy, do-it-yourself manner.

> Friend, our inside _and_ our outside matters. God says so.

Minding My Own Business

I believe in the depths of my heart that it's my calling to get women of faith everywhere feeling and looking their best and not feeling guilty about it. I remember sitting in my favorite chair one day, having quiet time and journaling. I was minding my own business, praying my usual prayers, when *it* happened. I heard God whisper. It was as clear as any other time He's spoken to me. No, you wouldn't have heard it; it wasn't audible. But in my spirit I felt something tug at my heart as clear as day.

I looked over at my husband who was engaged in his favorite night-time activity (you know, channel surfing), and I asked him to stop what he was doing and listen to me. He did. Then I told him what God said and waited anxiously for my hubby's response. He didn't blink, he didn't laugh, he didn't even pause. He just said, "Then you need to do it."

That night I knew God wanted me to take my knowledge of the fashion and beauty industry and go tell women inside church walls that it was okay to care about the way they looked. For a while, I argued with God and told Him I couldn't do it. But I protested for only seven years. I prayed, I hesitated. I prayed, I questioned. Then I prayed some more, and one day I finally took the first step. Here I am today, telling you what you've always wanted to know about fashion, personal style, and beauty, but didn't know where to turn for the answers.

God wants you to know that you are beautiful exactly as you are. You may be a size 6, a size 16, or a size 26. You may be a size 0, a size 10, or a size 20. Whatever your size, you are in the body God gave you ... and it is good. That is the message God wants you to hear and, more importantly, live out.

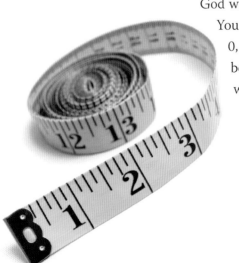

What's the Christian Fuss?

Clothes are clothes, makeup is makeup, and haircuts are haircuts, right? So why this separate Christian thing?

Because first and foremost, you need to know that "the king is enthralled by your beauty" (Ps. 45:11). Think about that for a minute! The King of the universe thinks you are amazing! He thinks you have the perfect size feet for your body. He thinks your nose fits your face exactly the way it should. He even gives you cellulite on your thighs to remind you of His fingerprints! Pretty cool, huh? (Well, I'm not sure that's the reason we have cellulite, but that's the way I like to think of it! After all, it's all about perspective.) Those hips you are always complaining about? Well, He made them for you. Whether you are blonde or brunette, Caucasian or African American, Indian or Asian, tall or petite, heavy or thin — I believe that when you get to heaven, you are going to find out that God's idea of perfect beauty is exactly what you look like.

Perfect beauty in God's eyes is not what I look like or what your sister, your child's teacher, or your college roommate looks like. It's about what *you* look like. Soak your spirit in that thought. Until you understand that concept, I mean, really get it, you will never fully understand why God expects you to care about your appearance.

Second, as a Christian you have a great responsibility. You are a representative of Jesus. To some, you may be the only representative they'll ever see. Hmmm. How does that make you feel? Are you confident that your outer appearance reflects who you are on the inside? In other words, is your inside beauty displayed on the outside?

Think of yourself as a package, a beautiful package for Christ! If given a choice, would you pick a present wrapped in old newspaper or one lovingly and carefully adorned with shiny gold paper and a spectacular bow? The answer, of course, is obvious. The point is, we should all want to present ourselves looking sharp and put-together.

Third, as a Christian you have a responsibility to be modest. Now don't go thinking that modesty is old-fashioned, boring, and fuddy-duddy. Modesty is taking care not to cause our brothers in Christ to sin in their minds, and oftentimes, in their actions. It's caring that you don't show your thong underwear to the cashier when you bend over in the convenience store. It's wearing the correct bra for certain clothing. It's not dressing so sexy that you attract the wrong kind of attention and therefore present the wrong message. Modesty shows others the type of person you are. The way you dress shows what's going on … on the inside of you.

So Now What?

Remember how I told you about the day God told me to take this message to women within the church? I wasn't wrestling with the decision because I didn't want to do it. I wrestled with it because I didn't know if the church would want me. I knew women everywhere were hungering for this sort of information. But I was so afraid of what I would be up against with the powers-that-be within the church walls. Why in the world would they invite me to speak to the women in their congregation when my topic was "outer" beauty? I knew God told me to do it, but could I convince anyone else of that?

And then something happened. A friend who had been praying with me about my situation invited me to speak at her church for a women's event. At that event there was a coordinator from an out-of-state church … so what do you think happened next? You got it! I was invited to her church. And on and on it went. God was walking before me, lining everything up because He knew His daughters were hurting in the beauty department. Now don't get me wrong; He thought they were fabulous the way they were, but they didn't know that. And He wanted me to tell them. He wanted me to do it in a way where they would leave my conferences and workshops equipped with the tools and knowledge to look and feel better about how to portray their God-given natural beauty.

Amy's Story

Dear Shari, my name is Amy. It has been some time since I gave a second thought to what I put on my body, and I really thought that it was in some women's nature to dress up while others of us are wired toward jeans and our husband's T-shirts. To be honest, I was skeptical at best, to see exactly what fashion had to do with my walk with God. Thank you for showing me that what I put on is a reflection of how I feel about myself, and how I feel about myself is a reflection of how I think I am viewed by God. He created me beautiful, and I realize now that He wants me to feel that way. I am the example my ten-year-old daughter sees every day of a godly woman, and I didn't realize that how I present myself is part of that. I realized that my example will affect how my daughter sees herself as a young woman, and your words will help me relay the message of beauty and fashion to her. My eyes have been opened to this wonderful message from God in such a loving, humorous, non-threatening way. I'm going to start putting things in my closet that allow the outside of me to shine as brightly as the light inside. After all, I am God's masterpiece and He expects me to be the best I can be.

I share Amy's message with you to make you think. You may be a jeans and T-shirt sort of girl who couldn't care less about clothes (even though you've convinced yourself of that, here you are reading this book!), or you may be a trend addict who buys every new style that comes out regardless of whether or not it's age appropriate or figure flattering.

Maybe you're still in college and even though you wear your favorite jeans to class, you want to know how to dress for the weekends and yet not look like a sex object. Or, like many women, you're a busy wife and mom who needs basic fashion guidance. Maybe you are a twenty- or thirty-something single woman who spends a lot of money on unnecessary clothes and it's finally time to build a smart wardrobe. Or possibly, you're an empty nester, close to retirement, and need casual outfits that can take you to lunch, Bible study, volunteer commitments, and on weekend getaways.

Regardless of who you are or what stage of life you are in, we all have a need to feel beautiful. We all have a responsibility to take care of ourselves, and sometimes we just need a little guidance on how to do it. Hey, even Esther in the Bible prepared for a year to see the king by having beauty treatments! Some of you have trouble finding time for a bubble bath without feeling guilty.

Do Not Worry

I remember the day Lysa TerKeurst, president of Proverbs 31 Ministries, called me and told me she wanted to share something with me. She said she couldn't wait to tell me what the Lord had revealed to her that morning during her prayer time. She knew it was a message specifically for me.

Lysa was one of the very first people to believe that my ministry was important for women. The first time we ever spoke on the phone, she passionately agreed that Christian women were afraid to talk about outer appearance, and so it was a much needed and desired topic for discussion. She invited me to come and train the other speakers who were on her team on how to create a professional personal style. On the day she phoned to tell me about her revelation from the Lord, Lysa told me to go look up Matthew 6:25 – 32:

> Therefore I tell you, do not worry about your life, what you will eat or drink; or about your body, what you will wear. Is not life more important than food, and the body more important than clothes? Look at the birds of the air; they do not sow or reap or

store away in barns, and yet your heavenly Father feeds them. Are you not much more valuable than they? Who of you by worrying can add a single hour to his life? And why do you worry about clothes? See how the lilies of the field grow. They do not labor or spin. Yet I tell you that not even Solomon in all his splendor was dressed like one of these. If that is how God clothes the grass of the field which is here today and tomorrow is thrown into the fire, will he not much more clothe you, O you of little faith? So do not worry, saying, What shall we eat? Or What shall we drink? Or What shall we wear? For the pagans run after all these things and your heavenly Father knows that you need them."

The point she wanted me to take away was for me to see that this passage is not giving us instruction on "what to wear" (or what not to wear), but giving us instruction on "not to worry." Many people take these verses to mean that we shouldn't be bothered by the seemingly small stuff, like finding the right outfit or getting the perfect hairstyle. Those things in and of themselves aren't bad. I believe that we can run into a problem when we start obsessing over our looks, when we solely focus our attention on the outside — like looking perfect — instead of working on our inner beauty. God wants you to look good, as beautiful as the lilies of the field, and as splendid as King Solomon in all his glory. But He doesn't want you to get bogged down by the obsession, and He doesn't want you to worry.

God wants you to take care of yourself.

Beauty in All the Wrong Places

I'm going to let you in on a secret.

God wants you to take care of yourself. Remember what the apostle Paul told the Corinthians: "Do you not know that your body is a temple of the Holy Spirit, who is in you, whom you have received from God? . . . Therefore honor God with your body." (1 Cor. 6:19 – 20). Now, that's a big revelation! Okay, so you may have heard it before, but do you really believe it? God tells us to honor our bodies and to take care of ourselves.

God also thinks you're pretty cute! The reality is that most of us don't think we are. We've decided that we'd look better as a blonde, so we dye our hair. We'd really like a smaller nose, bigger breasts, thinner thighs, higher cheekbones, curly or straight hair (whichever we don't have), a flatter tummy, and a tiny rear, so we do whatever it takes to get there. We start searching out the answers to our issues (or paying for surgery), and end up deciding that everyone else is prettier, thinner, and taller than us, so why even bother?

Beauty is not what you think it is. Beauty is not where you think it is. Beauty is you. Beauty is me. We are beauty. Beauty is God. What do I mean? Beauty is in the natural. It's not about airbrushing or tons of makeup or plastic surgery. Beauty is already found in us in its natural form before we ever mess with it. One of my favorite passages in the Bible is Psalm 139:14: "I praise you because I am fearfully and wonderfully made; your works are wonderful, I know that full well."

I especially love the last part of that verse, "I know that full well."

I don't believe it's any accident that you've chosen to read this book. I've been praying for you during the entire writing process. I believe the thing that God wants you to know the most when you are finished is just what the verse above states. You will be able to look at your body and know, full well, that you are fearfully and wonderfully made. The exciting part is, even though we can't all have a perfect body (whatever that is), you are about to embark on a fashion and beauty adventure. I'll be your guide as you learn that God didn't make a mistake with you, and you can dress your outer appearance with newfound confidence.

I'm going to help you have confidence in how to dress, how to make up your face, how to accessorize, and how to build a wardrobe. I'm going to help you believe in yourself so you can put together outfits that are perfectly coordinated. You won't worry about what you look like in them because you will know they look terrific on you. You are

Beauty is you.
Beauty is me.
We are beauty.
Beauty is God.

Introduction:

about to become a junior fashionista! And hey, if you already are one, you'll gain even more knowledge that you can share with all of your friends.

Are you ready to get started? Are you ready to stop screaming, "Help me, Jesus! I have nothing to wear!"?

Now go stand in front of a mirror. Take a deep breath. Smile, look straight ahead, and realize that … *You* are the woman in that mirror. *You* are a Christian. *You* have permission to take care of your outer appearance.

So, how do you look?

Gorgeous, I say. Absolutely gorgeous.

This Is My Bod:
Determine Your Real Body Type

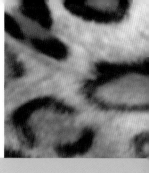

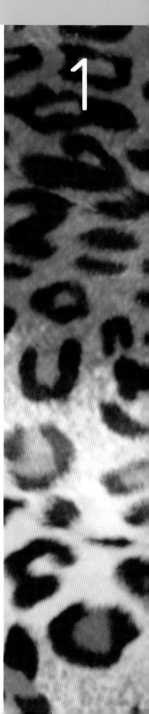

HERE'S AN EMAIL I RECEIVED WHEN I FIRST BEGAN SPEAKING IN churches all over the country. Jeanne, a woman from Michigan, wrote:

> *I have always felt that I could never really look good in clothes because I am short and I can never find clothes to fit me properly. What I didn't understand was that I was buying clothes that didn't work for my body shape. After you taught me about my body type and the correct styles to look for, I have a whole new outlook on my wardrobe. Although learning about my shape was a little intimidating at first, it ended up being a very eye-opening and life-changing experience.*

I Love My Body!

Does the idea of discussing your body type cause you to break into a cold sweat? If I asked you to do an assessment of your body, would you list more things you like about how you look or more things you hate about your appearance? For most women, like Jeanne, learning and talking about their body can be quite a harrowing experience. The reason is obvious.

Many of us are dissatisfied with our bodies. We don't like our thighs. We don't like our stomachs. We don't like our waists. Some of us even have a problem with our knees. Many of us cringe at the number on the size tags of our clothes. Are we really a size ___?

Before I can tell you how to determine your body type and then teach you the best way to dress it up, there is something you have to do first. Something all of us have to do. We have to let go of our hang-ups about our bodies. I know it's not easy. I know it won't happen overnight.

Loving and accepting your body is one of the core truths behind this book. To want to look your best is to first look at yourself and admire God's handiwork. Not to moan that your body doesn't look like that of the latest Hollywood "It" girl.

Worship God by loving and caring for your body.

Intermixed with this principle is the idea that because our body belongs to the Lord, we should care for it and love it the way God would want us to.

I was reminded of this through something that happened to my husband. Some time ago, he came down with a nasty respiratory infection that put him in the hospital. I was worried about him and couldn't sleep one night. It was also his birthday. I got to thinking about the condition of his health and his body, and then I got to thinking about mine.

You see, I typically fluctuate between a size 12 and 14. And I am quite alright with it. Seriously. I'm not kidding you. In fact, I think I've even come to be proud of it. Are your eyes bugging out as you think, "Whaaaaat?"

Yes, dear reader, I'm proud of my size. 'Cause really, I don't think I look like it. Now I might to others, but I've completely convinced myself I'm thin. I figure if I think I look alright, then who cares what anyone else thinks!

As I tossed and turned, I kept on thinking. I stand in front of hundreds of women every single weekend and tell them my height (5'11") and my size. I do that so women will honestly know that beauty is not about the size of our clothes. We are not a reflection of the number on that tag. God gave us exactly the body He wants us to have, the exact frame size, and everything else that goes along with that. We are made in His image, and we are all so incredibly beautiful.

As I thought about my husband in the emergency room, I realized that we all need to pay better attention to our health. The way I look at it, I can be a fluffy size 14 or I can be a firm size 14. And maybe firming up will make me a size 12, and that's okay too. The point is to be healthy.

Now I'm not talking about doing things in an unrealistic, obsessive, or unhealthy way, like crash dieting or exercising four hours a day. I'm talking about making better choices when it comes to our health. There are two simple things we can do to take a step in the right direction: Eat better and exercise. Like I've said before, we have a responsibility to our Lord. He wants us to accept our bodies, be grateful for them, and know we are gorgeous inside and out. And He also wants us to take care of those bodies, from the smallest of us to the largest of us.

So as you dive into learning about your individual body type and as you read through this book, remember to love yourself and take care of yourself. Doing that is one way of thanking God for creating you! Unique and special you!

The Perfect Body

Throughout this book I'm going to ask you to do a number of things, from looking at yourself through new eyes to shopping with a new mind-set. I hope you'll take me up on the activities and challenges I suggest because any time we make a change, it always begins with movement. Will you do this?

Here's your first assignment: Take a good look at your body. You might not have done this in a very long time and it may be difficult for you to see yourself objectively, but you need to do it. Make sure you are observing yourself in front of a full-length mirror, if possible.

What do you like about your body? What are some of your great attributes? Perhaps you like your athletic build, your curvy waistline, or the shape of your arms. List a few of those things here:

_____

_____

_____

I know this first task may not have been that easy, so here's something else for you to do: Write down some of your body's challenges. Specifically think about where you gain your weight. Does your extra fluffiness (it's not fat anymore, girls, it's fluff!) show up in your tummy, your hips and thighs, your upper body and bust area, or do you pretty much gain weight evenly all over? List those trouble spots here:

The perfect body is a well-balanced body.

_____

_____

_____

You may be one of those women who does not have trouble with weight gain and has a somewhat balanced body. This brings me to the idea of the "perfect body." What does that mean for you? In America, it seems the perfect body is over 5'10" and a size 4. Think supermodels, celebrities, and the airbrushed women you see gracing the cover pages of fashion and beauty magazines.

Looking your best means knowing what your body shape is and dressing for it so your body looks proportional. That's what this is all about. It's not about looking like a beanpole (and if you do, that's okay too); it's about making your body seem perfectly proportional. You don't have to camouflage the body parts you don't like. Instead, you can dress so those parts look better balanced with the rest of your body.

It's time to stop throwing on an oversized tunic. It's time to stop wrapping a bulky sweater around your waist. It's time to stop wearing sweat suits every single day because you think it's the only thing that will cover you up. It's time to dress balanced!

Let's get back to your body assessment. If you are completely honest with yourself, your body really isn't all bad, is it? I bet you have a few challenges, but once you understand how you can make them look better, you might not mind them anymore.

The bod-x System

There are four specific body shapes we're going to discuss. Wherever you gain weight determines your body type. I'm sure you've heard all kinds of names for body shapes, from pears and apples to squares and rectangles. They're all good, but for our purposes I'm going to be referring to them by the bod-x system. Most women gain the majority of their weight in one of four places:

- Tummy
- Upper midriff and bust
- Booty and hips/thigh area
- Even gain all over

Are you nodding your head already, knowing exactly where you fit in? This correlates exactly with what you have identified as your trouble spots above. It is possible to gain weight in multiple areas, such as in your tummy *and* your hips. If this is the case, then you are a combination of types and you'll want to follow the guidelines for both.

The following few pages contain a description of each of the body types. Check off those traits that describe you and note where you have the most checks. This will be your body type. Generally speaking, if you gain your weight primarily in your belly, you are a b body type. The o body is the overly endowed, busty gal and may gain weight in her tummy and upper midriff. The d body will gain her weight in her derrière, hips, and thighs, and the x body will have a balanced figure, whether she is at her ideal weight or not.

Body Type b

- Balanced shoulders and hips
- Gains weight in belly
- Fuller waist or muffin top
- Straight figure
- Not too much in the rear

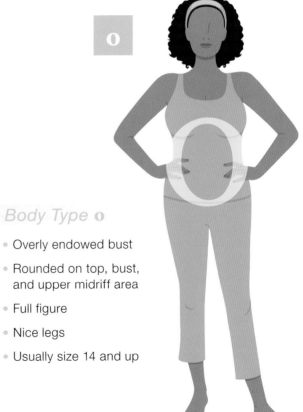

Body Type o

- Overly endowed bust
- Rounded on top, bust, and upper midriff area
- Full figure
- Nice legs
- Usually size 14 and up

This Is My Bod:

Body Type **d**

- Gains weight in hips, thighs, and derrière
- Narrow waist
- Small- to medium-width shoulders
- Minimal bustline
- Full bottom

Body Type **x**

- Shoulders and hips are balanced
- Narrow waist
- Gains weight evenly all over
- Ideal weight
- Balanced proportions

Which body type are you? Circle one of the letters below.

b o d - x

Which body shape best describes you? Which one has the most check marks?

Keep in mind the bod-x system is not an exact science. It's like a compass that points you in the general direction of the kind of proportions you have. My job is to tell you what you can do to make every part look its best.

The reason it's important to know our challenge areas is that, even though God did not make a blunder with giving you the type of body you have, we can better understand, appreciate, and make our challenge areas appear less obvious.

As you think about your body type and determine which letter you are, don't be discouraged. If you are a b, don't wish you were an x. If you are a d, don't start belittling your booty. Don't be so hard on yourself. Be kind. Love every inch of you. Accept who you are. Appreciate the uniqueness with which you were made. And be thankful you don't look like everyone else. Wouldn't life be dull if we all looked the same?

Keep reading and go to the heading labeled with your identified body type. Get to know how to dress to look balanced. Oh, and for you x's, just because you're more balanced than the rest of us, don't stop reading. Continue on to your section. Even x's have some challenge areas every now and then. Occasionally an x develops into a different body type, so you may want to learn about the other body types as they apply.

> *I am a stay-at-home mom and I struggle with knowing what clothes to buy so I can look nice, yet not spend too much money since we live on a pretty tight budget. I definitely don't always put the effort in every day to get out of my sweats, but after hearing you at our church conference, I know I need to do a better job at that. I am trying to learn the "rules" for my body type so I can look my best. I am totally inspired to do it!*
>
> *Jennifer*

This Is My Bod:

b Body Type

If you are a b, then your challenge area is your belly. You may wish that you had a little more junk in your trunk, but hey, it's not the end of the world. There are many women out there who would trade their shape for yours. Here are some tips that will help you accentuate your body and make you look great.

Never tuck in your tops. This is a definite no-no. Whenever you tuck shirts in, attention is immediately drawn to the tummy area. Use caution with belts. Don't wear them around your waist, as this will draw attention to the area you are trying to hide. If you want to wear a belt, make it a wider one that is slung low across your tummy at an angle. It's kind of a funky look (in a trendy way) and will disguise the trouble spot.

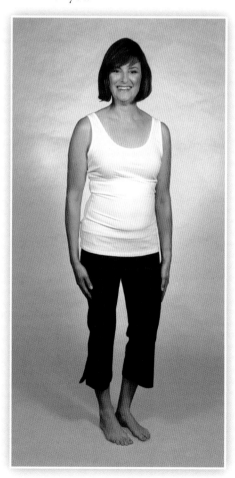

The shirts and jackets you wear should always cover the fullest part of your body. The perfect place for them to fall is just below your tummy. Stay away from short jackets that hit at the waistline or just below the waist. Stick with a longer length jacket that falls right above the hips. You can even try a duster type that hits just above the knees.

Accessorize! Accessorize! Accessorize! Do this especially at the neckline. It's a great way to draw attention away from your middle and toward your face and neck. Don't be afraid of chunky necklaces.

Nix the shoulder pads. I know this is very 1980's-esque, but styles always come back. For you, this style should be one you never indulge in. The great part about your shape is that your shoulders are

already balanced with your hips. You've got that great proportion going for you. If you purchase clothes with shoulder pads already attached, take them out and throw them away.

Stay away from slacks with pleated fronts. This will make your midsection appear bigger than it is. Flat front or side zip slacks are a better option. Relaxed fit or full leg trousers are great for a b body type. A b looks best in monochromatic dressing with solids of colors near matching. Try wearing longer scarves and drape them in the front of your body.

A tummy shaper is a must-have item in your wardrobe. As with all body types, make sure you are properly fitted for the right bra. We'll talk about these two things later on.

It's very important for a b to wear the correct size, especially as it concerns tops. If you wear a shirt a size too small, it will cling to your tummy and make this challenge area appear bigger.

Column dressing — wearing three pieces of clothing like a shirt, a jacket, and pants — is a great way to appear slimmer. To create a column for a b, match the color of your inside pieces (the top and pants are the inside pieces, while the jacket is the outside one) or keep them near the same hue.

This Is My Bod:

Determine Your Real Body Type

This Is My Bod:

o Body Type

Whenever you're having one of those days when you wish your body wasn't so "upwardly blessed," remember there are a lot of women who'd like a little of what you have. As a matter of fact, many of these women are running to the nearest plastic surgeon to get it.

The most important item in your wardrobe is your bra. You have got to have it fit properly (see chapter 4 for more details). A good bra is necessary for all body types, but your health particularly depends on it; you can suffer from back problems with a heavy bust. The right bra will be an amazing asset to your body. You'll be surprised when you see the difference between an ill-fitted bra and one that is the right fit.

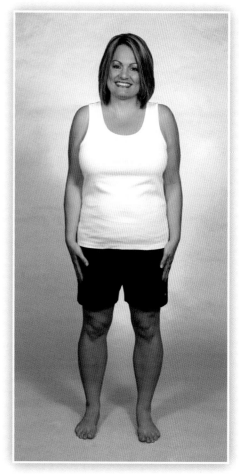

You most likely have great legs. Don't be shy. Don't hide them. Show them off! Go ahead and wear a shorter length skirt that falls right at the knee. This is a very classic look and flatters everyone, but especially you. As far as pants, look for ones that have only a slight flare to them. You don't want to look boxy by wearing slacks that are too full or wide at the bottom.

Jackets look fabulous on you. Stay away from ones that fit snug around your bosom. Always give your bust some breathing room. You will want to wear a ¾-length sleeve, so push your sleeves up if your jacket has long ones. A swing jacket is a timeless piece that will flatter you marvelously! This type of jacket is not a straight fit but has a little flare at the bottom. It almost looks as if it is swinging ... hence the name.

You will probably not be tucking many tops in,

Determine Your Real Body Type

but if you do, make sure you don't wear wide belts. Stick with the skinny ones.

Prints make a full bust appear smaller. When wearing solids, add a jacket to your outfit to minimize your upper body.

Because you have a beautiful bustline, you need to pay extra attention to how it looks. Be modest. Don't show them off to everyone around you. Leave your cleavage at home behind closed doors. Camisoles should be a staple in your wardrobe since so many tops seem to be low cut. You'll want to have plenty

on hand so you don't look like you are putting your bustline on display for the world to see. When you wear necklaces, be sure they don't fall on or into the bustline.

Similar to a b, column dressing works great for o's. This body type needs to build its column with the inside pieces as described on page 32. Remember, column dressing happens when you wear three pieces of clothing and two of the three are the same or near the same color.

This Is My Bod:

d Body Type

Calling all d's, calling all d's! I can already hear your frustration, girl-friend. I bet you have a tough time finding a pair of pants that fit both your hips and your waist, right? This is the biggest complaint I hear from d's. You know what? You probably never will, although some manufacturers are beginning to address this issue. Though that's the bad news, there is good news. You probably have a tailor in your neigh-borhood who can fix this problem for you. Buy pants that fit your hips and you can have someone take in the waist area. Voilà! Problem solved! When buying pants, make sure they have a flared leg at the bottom. The flare will always balance your hips, so keep plenty of them in your wardrobe.

If you don't want to have your pants altered, there is another solution called *isABelt*™. This is a thin, strong, and flexible clear plastic belt that virtually disappears when worn. It provides you with the assurance that all is secure without even knowing it's there. *isABelt* pre-vents back gap and slippage, making it perfect for the d body type. You can find one at www.isABelt.com for under $20. It may become your new best friend!

Be careful not to wear pants or skirts that hug your hips and thighs. All this does is make you look bottom heavy, something you are trying to avoid. Stay away from wearing patterned clothing below the waist. Keep patterns on top to draw attention to your upper half. Skinny jeans are not for you; don't be tempted to wear them, even if they are in style.

Short jackets look great on you as long as you wear

a flared or full skirt or slacks. Stay away from V-neck tops because, even though they make the other body types appear slimmer, they make you look like your upper body is disappearing. Opt for scoop or square necks. Blouses with collars look great on you too, as it creates a more balanced look. Off-the-shoulder styles are wonderful in the summertime since they add width where you need it most. Also, you can wear horizontal stripes on top.

An important item for you to own is a pair of shoulder pads you can take in and out of your tops. Some of you may be groaning right now. I know, I know, you hate shoulder pads. You probably think they are so yesterday and have always ripped them out of whatever tops you buy. It's time to put them back in ... and quick! Shoulder pads will never be out of style for a d because they actually help you out. These pads balance your hips and thighs and make you look more proportioned. It's a fact. Swing by a department or fabric store. Most of them sell shoulder pads. Buy the kind that can easily slip in and out of most outfits so you don't have to bother with a needle and thread.

Belts look amazing on you as they show off your cute waist. There is a huge assortment out there, from very thin to extra wide. Try all of them on and choose ones that suit your personal style.

Accessories are a must for you. Be playful. Be daring. Be bold. Throw on a bangle or two. Wear those big hoop earrings. Have some fun with accessories. The goal for you is to draw attention upward, so get creative with necklaces.

Choose colors wisely, d's. Be careful when wearing two different colors at the same time. For example, if your jacket is red and your slacks are black, you will have drawn the eye right to your challenge area as the jacket stops right at your fullest part. Make sure you don't cut yourself off. Think more monochromatically. Wear both a black jacket and black slacks with a contrasting blouse (red, for example) to draw the eye up and away from your bottom half. This is how you column dress and appear thinner; you create a vertical line with your outside pieces (jacket and slacks, for example).

This Is My Bod:

This Is My Bod:

x Body Type

Most consider you to have the perfect body type. Some will hate you, some will love you, but I'm sure you can get used to it! An x body type is very balanced and, therefore, may have a hard time finding clothes that fit all areas of the body. Did you know that many clothing manufacturers have a tendency to make clothes for an unbalanced body? Unfortunately, this is a problem for you. For instance, a suit might fit great in the jacket but may be too small in the skirt, or vice versa. Find a great tailor who can do some altering for you. Call a local men's store and see if they allow outsiders to use their services. Usually you can get expert work at a fair price.

You can wear a straight leg pant or jean better than anyone can. Wear them with a higher heel or boot and a sharp jacket or a loose-style top. Fuller tops always look better over skinnier bottoms. The same goes if you are wearing a full leg pant; pair it with a more fitted top. Skinny jeans are fabulous on you, so go for it, girl!

Most styles of clothing will look good on you, but pay attention to your frame size. If you have a small frame, you can easily look overpowered by prints or accessories that are too large. Or, you can overpower your accessories and prints if you have a medium to large frame and are wearing accessories on the small side. Belts of all kinds and sizes will look terrific on you, so wear them with confidence.

Be very careful that you don't appear overly sexy or sloppy. If your

This Is My Bod:

clothes are too tight, you may look sexy when it's not appropriate. If your clothes are too big, you will look like you don't care about your appearance. Drawing attention to the center of your body is always a

good tip to look your best, so use column dressing by creating a longer line with your clothes. Wear colors that are similar in hue so there is no breaking point. Add colorful accessories to bring attention inward and upward toward your face.

Make a point of getting a proper bra fitting. It will make all the difference in the way you look in your clothes.

Celebrate your fabulous body and keep an eye on it as you age and things start to move around. You may find yourself at some point seeking wisdom from a b or a d.

Celebrating Curves

Curves are good. Really, they are. If you are a full-figured beauty, then this section is written just for you. Most of us were never meant to be a size 2 or 4, so please stop comparing yourself to those God *did* make that way. When I described each of the four body shapes, you may have found yourself not fitting into just one type, but a combination of them. This is typical for a full-figured gal. It's most important to understand your body and how to balance your figure with your clothes. I'd suggest you put on leggings or workout pants and a camisole and stand in front of a mirror. Do a 360 and check out your body from all angles. Where exactly are your challenge areas? Are you an x that gains weight evenly all over? Or a b that gains mostly in her tummy? Perhaps you feel like you are all boobs. Then you'd be an o. Got it all in the hips, thighs, and booty? Then the letter d is yours. One of my blog readers recently commented (when we were discussing body types) that she thought she was a "hybrid" x/o body shape! I laughed out loud when I read it. It seemed to catch on and reader after reader kept describing herself as a "hybrid" something or other! So maybe you're a hybrid; what a fun way to look at it.

No matter your body shape, or combination thereof, make sure you dress to flatter your gorgeous figure. When you do that, it doesn't matter what size you are, you will always look and feel great.

When choosing a pant style, stay with a more relaxed leg as this will balance your body better than

This Is My Bod:

This Is My Bod:

something very wide or very narrow. Skinny jeans will make you look top heavy so beware of those.

Stay away from too-tight clothes. There is nothing worse than seeing a beautiful friend in clothes that hug her body too closely. We always look slimmer and more attractive in clothes that fit well. If something "just" fits, then I go up one size. Trust me on this. On the other hand, don't wear too big, sloppy clothes either. Just because you are a hybrid doesn't mean you can go around trying to cover it all up. Remember, hybrids are the newest thing on the market, and they are the best dressed things in the showrooms — so don't go hiding in the back room or rather, under a bunch of fabric.

Patterns are okay as long as they are worn according to your scale. See the chapter on accessorizing for more information on this. If you are a petite full-figured gal, then go more medium on your prints, not too large or small. For some reason, most plus sized clothing lines seem to use a lot of stripes. Why is that? Stripes aren't bad as long as they are not wide ones. Make sure your stripes are close together if they are horizontal ones. Vertical stripes are fine.

Be careful with short jackets. A jacket that comes just below the fullest part on your tummy will be the best length for you. Swing jackets are fabulous on you too, but be careful with too-long jackets as it may appear you are all "upper body" and you don't want to look like you are about to fall over!

V-necks and blouses with embellishments near your neckline are a wonderful way to bring attention to the center of your body and to your face. Buy these all day long.

Belts are a no-no for you. Now, having said this, if you still choose to wear a belt, make sure it is worn on an angle and slung low. We just don't want to decorate our fluff, you know? And belts tend to do this. No one with a tummy issue should wear a belt, so don't think you are the only one not doing so.

Accessories are a way to play up your unique style. Never go too small. Have fun with accessories, bags, jewelry, and scarves. Go bright, go bold. Show your style through unique pieces.

It's most important to understand your body and how to balance your figure with your clothes.

Color is one of the most important aspects to dressing. Make certain your wardrobe is filled with shades that make you glow. Monochromatic color dressing is a super slimming trick. Wear pieces similar in hue and add scarves or jewelry in contrasting colors to draw the on-looker's eye inward toward the center of your body. Column dressing is when you wear the same color top and bottom and a contrasting jacket or outer piece. Be careful when wearing two different colors at the same time (unless it's in a pattern or print). For example, if you have on chocolate denim jeans and a white top that ends at the fullest part of your tummy, you will draw attention to your stomach. Instead, make sure your top is longer than the fullest part of your belly OR wear a chocolate top (to match the brown jeans) to create a longer, leaner line. Throw on a patterned jacket or another solid color jacket and you've just created a column.

Above all, remember you are a fabulous full-figured woman, so dress with confidence.

Do you love your body a little more now? I hope so!

It takes some practice to know exactly what styles of clothing to look for, but as you learn to shop with a sharp eye, you will automatically start searching out styles that flatter your figure.

Now that you know what styles to look for, let's find out what colors are sure to flatter you.

This Is My Bod:

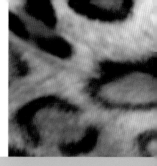

The Truth about Black:
Meet Your True Colors

LIKE MOST TEENAGE BOYS, MY SON LUKE ISN'T THAT INTO fashion. His outfit of choice is almost always a pair of athletic shorts and a T-shirt. That is as fashion forward as he gets. The one thing the kid knows, however, is color. He's got this uncanny knack for knowing exactly what color looks good or not so good on someone (must get it from his mother). My son also doesn't mind giving his opinion on "color analysis," even if he isn't asked for his thoughts.

Luke was the quarterback for his middle school football team. I remember watching one of his games and getting wrapped up in the moment, when out of nowhere two cheerleaders bounced up the bleachers toward me. Their faces were flushed with emotion and they looked exasperated. "Mrs. Braendel," they chorused, "Luke told us we don't look good in pink! Is that true?"

Oh boy! The funny thing was, the girls were genuinely concerned. They desperately wanted to know if Luke was right or not, but more importantly they wanted to know if they should never again wear pink. As it turned out, my son was right. Both girls had very warm coloring to their complexion and light reddish hair, so pink was a no-go. After I shared this with them, they were shocked. With horrified looks of, "Oh my gosh! We love pink and we'll never be able to wear it again!" they bounced down the bleachers and onto the sidelines.

Color Matters

Does color matter that much? It sure does. It matters as much as determining and dressing for your body type. As a matter of fact, knowing your colors is winning half the battle of dressing to look your best. You've already won the first half of the battle — body shape — in the last chapter. The natural color of our complexion, hair, and eyes determines whether particular colors make us look radiant or washed out, youthful or aged, energized or exhausted.

Now, color can be a tricky thing. Many of us have general misconceptions about what looks good and what doesn't. The biggest misunderstanding most women have is that black is a universal color. It should look great on everyone, right? After all, the dark hue is slimming, and all the hip people who work in trendy stores wear black all the time. It's cool. It's classic. So isn't it true that everyone should have, for instance, a basic black dress and slacks? Well, no.

There's more to life than black. Try to tell sales clerks that when their store is full of black clothes, and I promise you they'll protest that statement. But friend, you must trust me on this. Black doesn't flatter many women and, in fact, can help you look older than you are. Who needs help in that area? I certainly don't!

It's time for you to learn a new way of looking at color, as well as a new way of looking at you. And for some of you, by the time you finish reading this chapter, it might even be time for you to toss out or donate the millions of black pants and shirts you own.

Today was my first day of trying my "light" colors. A complete stranger commented to me during the day: "I like that look you have! What a great outfit!" With my new cream suit, I felt great. I've never worn a light suit in my life, only black. Wow! What a change!

Nancy

The Truth about Black:

Put Your Money Where Your Color Is

For a number of years, I owned an image consulting firm in Miami, Florida, and helped professional women of all ages look their best all the time. One day, I got an unusual phone call from an attorney who needed some advice, and fast. To be honest, I was flattered and chuckled to myself. Imagine that, an attorney calling ME for advice!

This woman was representing a client going through a divorce, and they were going to have to appear in court to finalize the proceedings. The client was hoping to receive a lot of money from her cheating husband, but there was a chance she wouldn't get a dime. Her husband could afford a much more expensive attorney known for winning divorce cases. This woman's attorney didn't beat around the bush. She asked me, "What color suit should my client wear to earn pity from the judge so she will be awarded a large amount of money to keep her children fed and clothed?"

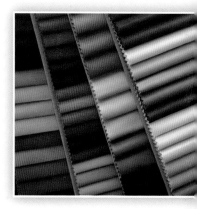

Wow! It was a loaded question. Because of my reputation in the image and fashion industry, she counted on me to have the right answer. Before I could give an educated response, I needed to find out a few things. I asked the attorney to tell me what her client looked like. What was the color of her hair, her complexion, the shade of her eyes? After we talked for a bit, I finally suggested that her client wear a suit in a muted shade of gray, as that was a very unflattering color for her.

Was I right? You betcha! I found out later that the woman going through the awful divorce case was awarded a very handsome sum of money. Now, I'm sure it didn't have everything to do with the shade of her suit, but still ... I'd like to think it helped.

Getting Back to the Basics

When I began to learn about color analysis, I received my schooling from Color Me Beautiful. Considered the premier color company, Color Me Beautiful began in the early eighties and took the fashion scene by storm with their color analysis system. I was taught that most women fell into four categories or, as the experts in the company liked to call them, seasons. Some of you may already be familiar with these terms. Depending on your dominant color characteristics, you were a winter, spring, summer, or autumn. It seemed simple enough.

A few years after my initial training, the company informed us that their original way of "doing" colors was being updated. They discovered that there were more than four kinds of coloring out there, and they needed to broaden their spectrum. So off I went to a new training workshop in Nashville, Tennessee, where, along with twenty-five other consultants, we were taught the new system.

At the beginning of the week I decided the trainers were crazy and the new method was even crazier. It seemed too complicated. I never thought I'd understand this new way of doing things. But a day or so into the workshop, I realized I would never look at women's coloring the same way again. The new system made sense and was actually very eye opening for me. There was a method to what I first thought was madness.

That was about twenty years ago. I've been using the method religiously ever since. In the last few years, however, I've tweaked it a bit. While Color Me Beautiful divided women into twelve categories, I decided it was better to put women into six categories and offer them more color choices. Believe me, it works. Every weekend I see several hundred to sometimes thousands of women at my *Fashion Meets Faith* Christian women's conferences and *Beauty Boot Camp*, and I've found my adapted color system to work marvelously.

See, I believe there are more color options for women than perhaps we have been led to believe. For instance, you may have been told that you could wear only silver or only gold accessories. In my experience,

I have found that most women can wear both. So why settle for one or the other if you don't have to?

Determining which colors look best (or worst) on you depends on your dominant color characteristics. This starts with your hair color. Are you a natural blonde, a vibrant redhead, or a medium brunette? Perhaps you have jet black, silver, or white hair.

But it doesn't stop there. We must then move to the shade of your eyes. Are they light or vibrant blue? Are they green or hazel? Are they deep brown or medium brown? Maybe yours are a greenish-blue.

We're still not finished. We finally move on to your skin tone. Are you fair skinned? A deep mocha? Do you tan or sunburn easily? Do you have more of a medium or a dark complexion?

Because I can't physically be with you, my web-designer husband (isn't God good to give me a man who could do this?) has created a program on my website to help you figure out your dominant color characteristics. Please visit www.FashionMeetsFaith.com and click on "Color E-nalysis" to find out the category that best suits you. This tool will lead you through a series of questions to get you to the proper category for your particular coloring. Once you have determined this, you can then understand the best colors for you and learn how these hues will help you to look your very best.

Thank you for the amazing workshop. What a difference color has already made! You pointed out to me that even though I shared the same hair and skin coloring as my best friend, the beige sweater I was wearing washed me out, whereas her fuchsia sweater made her look radiant. You made a believer out of me!

I had no idea the impact color can have. Sunday (at church) and yesterday (at work), I wore a purple top over a black dress and got rave reviews.

I am thrilled and amazed at the number of compliments I have already received. One coworker even commented that she never noticed I had blue eyes before!

Donna

Dominant Color Descriptions

There are six dominant color categories: Light, Deep, Soft, Clear, Warm, and Cool. Read each description as it pertains to your coloring and see where you belong. Whether you are taking this assessment here in this book or on my website at www.FashionMeetsFaith.com, the most important thing is to be honest. Be truthful about your coloring. What? Are you thinking you would never lie about that?

Here's the thing. Sometimes we look in the mirror and don't see ourselves accurately. We may think we are light blonde, when in fact we have lots of blonde highlights but our base hair color is medium brown. Or we may be dark auburn yet see ourselves with no red. Make sense? So for this part, it may be best to ask someone close to you what color they think you have and go with that. You might even want to do this with a few close friends so you can help each other out.

I used to ask women to begin with their natural coloring, but have found that most of us don't even know what that is anymore!

Are you ready to find the category that fits your dominant color characteristics?

I've scheduled an appointment with my hairdresser to return to the color closest to the one God gave me. Thank you for steering me in the right direction for the right reason — to better reflect the beauty of the King.

Karla

The Truth about Black

LIGHT

Naturally blonde hair or white hair (due to hair changing to this)

Fair skin tone

Light to medium eye color

DEEP

Medium to dark brown hair or black hair

Medium to dark skin tone

Hazel, brown, or black eyes

SOFT

Light to medium brown hair, sometimes described as mousy or dishwater blonde

Light to medium skin tone

Medium intensity eye color, like hazel, brown, blue, or green

CLEAR

Dark medium brown to black hair

Very fair to light or medium skin tone

Bright eye color (green, blue, or hazel) or dark brown

WARM

Red hair or golden blonde or brown hair with reddish highlights

Any skin tone, sometimes with freckles

Green, blue, brown, or hazel eyes

COOL

Silver, gray, or ash brown

Light to deep skin tone, most often with a pink undertone (but not always)

Blue, green, hazel, or brown eyes

New Colors ... New You

If you know for certain into which category you belong, then read on to get more detailed information about what colors suit you. There are thirty-six shades in each category that have been carefully selected to flatter each woman. I will also answer the following questions to help you make your daily color choices:

Color Intensity: What is the general range of colors you should wear?

Accessories: Should you wear silver or gold?

Best Neutrals: What are the neutral shades of color you should base your wardrobe around?

Pop Colors: What are the colors that help you to light up whenever you walk into a room?

White or Ivory: Should you wear one or the other?

The Truth about Black: Is it for you or not?

Best Shoe and Purse Color: What colors look best for these particular accessories?

Best Makeup Shades: What colors of cosmetics should you stick with?

Hair Advice: What can you do to enhance or maintain the best hair color for you?

Stay Away From: What colors should you never wear?

Even though this book will give you an idea of the colors, you may want to have your own personal "Color Swatch Shopping Guide" that you can keep in your purse for easy access when shopping. This shopping guide is a handy tool and includes fabric swatches so you know exactly what colors look best. I offer these swatches on my website. Visit www.FashionMeetsFaith.com to find out more information.

I always carry my swatches in the front pocket of my purse. You never know when a good shopping experience might present itself! You might think that I should know my best colors by now (especially since I've chosen all the colors for it!), but I don't trust the lighting in the department and specialty stores. Looking at my swatches versus relying on a store with poor lighting helps me know without a doubt I'm choosing the right colors.

Color Intensity: Pale to medium hues

Accessories: Silver and gold

Best Neutrals: Charcoal, navy, light camel

Pop Colors: Turquoise, pink, lavender, sapphire blue

White or Ivory: Either works for you

The Truth about Black: Beware of black as it will overpower you. Black works best with platinum blonde or all white hair.

Best Shoe and Purse Color: Because you are blonde or have white hair, my usual rule doesn't apply to you (matching your hair). Opt instead for light camel, taupe, or charcoal.

Best Makeup Shades: Pinks, roses, peaches, or neutrals

Hair Advice: Get highlights and lowlights if you want to enhance your natural coloring. Don't use an all-over color because it may look fake.

Stay Away From: Very dark or too bright colors; bold makeup is not for you.

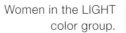
Women in the LIGHT color group.

Color Intensity: Medium to deep shades, some brights

Accessories: Silver and gold

Best Neutrals: Black or dark brown

Pop Colors: Purple, true red, persimmon, royal blue

White or Ivory: Both

The Truth about Black: Yes, it's for you! Anytime, anywhere!

Best Shoe and Purse Color: If your hair is medium to deep brown, choose dark brown for your best shoe and purse color. If your hair is dark brown to black, then choose black.

Best Makeup Shades: Browns, neutrals, berries

Hair Advice: Your dark natural hair is best, so when highlighting, don't go too light. Medium shades of caramel and toffee are great choices of highlights for you. Keep the highlights minimal around your face.

Stay Away From: Muted colors for clothes, and coloring your hair too light

Women in the DEEP color group.

The Truth about Black:

Color Intensity: Medium hues

Accessories: Silver and gold

Best Neutrals: Charcoal and medium brown

Pop Colors: Butter yellow, teal blue, coral, mint green

White or Ivory: Soft ivory

The Truth about Black: Never! Sorry, I know this really hurts your feelings, but black ages you and drains the color from your face.

Best Shoe and Purse color: Medium brown

Best Makeup Shades: Neutrals and browns with slight casts of pink or peach

Hair Advice: Highlights look beautiful on you, but be careful not to go too light or too dark. Always stay in the medium range of colors. You look best when you have several shades of highlights and lowlights. You can even add a little copper, but make sure it doesn't go too much to the red side or you'll end up in the Warm category.

Stay Away From: Black, black, and black! Oh, did I say black? Did I make it clear yet?! Also stay away from very bright colors and combinations of high contrast colors like black and white together.

Women in the SOFT color group.

CLEAR

Color Intensity: Bright hues

Accessories: Silver is best, but shiny gold works too

Best Neutrals: Black, navy, and deep charcoal gray

Pop Colors: Bright purple, clear red, sunny yellow, hot pink

White or Ivory: White

The Truth about Black: Yes for you! It looks especially great when worn with very light or very bright colors.

Best Shoe and Purse Color: Black

Best Makeup Shades: Vibrant shades of berry, fuchsia, and pink

Hair Advice: Stay as close to your natural hair color as possible. You are the only group who should never highlight your hair. Try a clear gloss to add some shine.

Stay Away From: Muted and dusty shades; beware especially of wearing brown and beige together.

Women in the CLEAR color group.

The Truth about Black:

Color Intensity: Hues with a yellow undertone, autumn-like shades

Accessories: Gold or silver/gold mix

Best Neutrals: Any shade of brown

Pop Colors: Rust, butterscotch, copper, turquoise

White or Ivory: Ivory

The Truth about Black: Not good on you, especially because chocolate brown is so much better. My advice? Move black out of your wardrobe or keep it only on the bottom half.

Best Shoe and Purse Color: Brown

Best Makeup Shades: Browns, neutrals, peaches, corals

Hair Advice: Stay red! If your color is starting to fade, add some beautiful copper highlights to give it a lift.

Stay Away From: Pink, pink, pink

Women in the WARM color group.

Color Intensity: Light to medium, but always with a blue or pink undertone

Accessories: Silver or rose gold

Best Neutrals: Black, navy, and gray

Pop Colors: Ocean blue, royal purple, blue-red, soft pink

White or Ivory: White

The Truth about Black: It's definitely for you!

Best Shoe and Purse Color: Black or charcoal

Best Makeup Shades: Pink, rose, berry, plum

Hair Advice: Keep it natural! Don't color it!

Stay Away From: Brown, beige, yellow, and orange

Women in the COOL color group.

The Truth about Black:

I had the most amazing experience with color last week after learning about the subject. I had the honor of going prom dress shopping with one of my BFFs and her daughter, Kaithlin. Kaithlin has red hair and very pale skin. When she tried on the copper colored dress I suggested, everyone in the dressing room area gasped! She looked like a princess.

Thanks for helping me make her day.

Amy

Now that you've learned about clothing styles that flatter your shape and colors that make you look radiant and polished, it's time to have a little fun. Bring out the bangles! Pull out the sunglasses! Show off those handbags! It's time to accessorize!

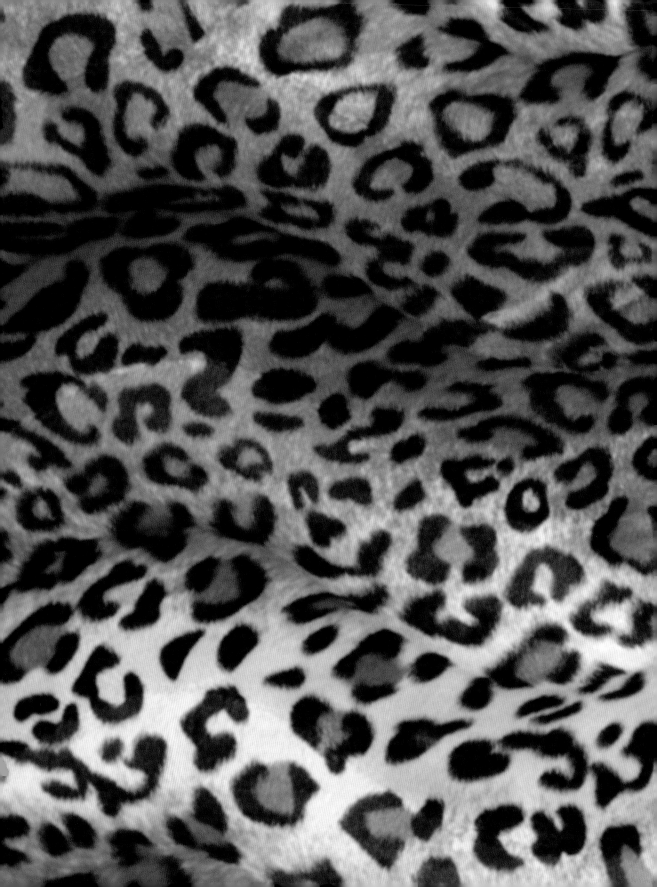

What's Your Score?

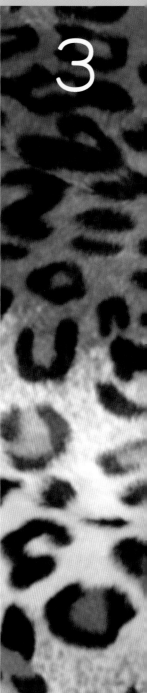

3

ONE OF THE THINGS I LIKE MOST ABOUT MIAMI IS PEOPLE-watching. Even though I no longer live there, I visit quite often. Every time I go, I make sure to sip a latte at a trendy South Beach café and admire the many beautifully dressed women as they strut by. While there are fashionable females in many parts of the country, I'd venture to say that those who visit from South America and shop in South Florida have to be some of the best-dressed women anywhere.

Years ago, I was the buyer and manager for the cosmetics department of a prominent specialty store in South Miami. Since the cosmetics counters in most stores are located near the entrance, I was able to see most of the customers enter and exit the building. Watching the way these women dressed, and particularly how they accessorized, became a sport to me. I observed. I studied. And I memorized the unique way in which these attractive women put themselves together. I noticed the size of their bracelets. I noticed the length of their necklaces. I noticed the height of their heels. I noticed the shape of their sunglasses. I noticed how many rings they had on. I noticed everything about them — what I liked and what I didn't.

People-watching is not just something fun to do to pass the time. You can learn a lot from it, especially when it comes to fashion. I actually credit much of my good taste and know-how in clothing and accessorizing to minding how those women in Miami adorned their outfits.

The next time you go somewhere and have the opportunity to sip on a cappuccino or simply rest your feet, keep an eye out for some chic women. Take a look at what they are wearing and how they put together their unique look. Without a doubt, the thing they will have in common will be their ability to accessorize.

It's More Than Just Throwing on a Necklace

Here's the thing: Most women don't know how to accessorize and finish what they've started. If you are going to dress in the most flattering way (like I've taught you in the first chapter), you need to add accessories. This subject may overwhelm some of you. I know the feeling. Many women come up to me during my workshops, very confused about the whole accessory topic. They ask me things like, "I don't want to buy too much jewelry, so how do I accessorize?" "How many accessories are enough?" "What kind of accessories should I wear?" "How do I know my accessories match my outfit?" No worries. I'm going to clear the air.

First, accessorizing is a wonderful thing. Think of it in terms of expressing yourself. Do you know that you have a very unique style? Perhaps you don't think so. Maybe you are so wrapped up in wearing sweatshirts and stretch pants all day that you're pretty certain you've lost the accessorizing touch. Or maybe you don't feel you even had it to begin with. I truly believe that there is an inner accessorizer in all of you. That's right. Each and every one of you. What makes me so confident to say that?

It's simple. I'd venture to say that you like what you like. There are pieces of clothing and styles that you are fond of, and then there are those that you would never wear even if someone paid you to. In other words, you have style. That's

What's Your Score?

right! And learning how to correctly accessorize is a way for you to channel that inner you.

Second, what exactly are accessories? This may seem to have an obvious answer to some of you, but others may not be entirely sure. When it comes to accessorizing, most women think in terms of jewelry. But guess what? It doesn't stop there. There are handbags, scarves, glasses, shoes, and other things that can pull your outfit together. Like the title of this section, accessorizing doesn't just mean throwing on a necklace. It can mean wearing Jackie O – type sunglasses and a chunky belt. It can mean having your nails done and wrapping a printed shawl over your blouse. It can mean so many things!

Most women don't know how to accessorize and finish what they've started.

How Much Is Enough?

Before we walk through the different accessories and I give you some pointers on what type of things look good on your body frame, let me answer the question I get asked most at my conferences and workshops: Exactly how many accessories are enough? Here's a great way to help you gauge whether you are wearing the right amount.

Somewhere along the road of my career in fashion, I learned about the "16 Point Accessory Rule." (I hate not to give credit where credit is due, but I simply can't remember where I learned this system.) This is a method where you add (or subtract) points for exactly what you are wearing. The object is to reach sixteen points when you are finished.

The 16-Point Accessory Rule

Are you ready to count? Let's get started at your shoes and head upward. Give yourself:

_____ One point for each of your shoes

_____ One point if you have a pretty pedicure and it is showing because of open-toe shoes

_____ One point if you have on fashionable tights or leggings (no points for regular pantyhose)

_____ One point for each garment you have on. If your garment has more than two colors, give yourself an additional point. For example, if you have on black jeans, a black jacket, and a multi-colored blouse, you get 4 points total (one point each for your jeans and jacket, and two points for the multi-colored blouse).

_____ One point if you are wearing a belt

_____ One point for each of your rings (wedding ring sets receive one point for the complete set)

_____ One point each for any watch, bracelet, or bangle

_____ One point for a necklace (if your necklace has a double or triple strand or is very large, give yourself two points)

_____ One point for each of your earrings

_____ One point if you are wearing glasses

_____ One point if you have makeup on

_____ One point if you've had a compliment on your hair in the last two weeks (more about this in chapter 6)

_____ One point for nice nails (They don't have to be professionally manicured, but they do have to look taken care of. No chipped polish, please.)

_____ One point for your handbag if you will be carrying it 100 percent of the time; if not, don't give yourself a point

_____ One point for a shawl, hat, scarf, wrap, or other add-on accessory item

That's it! Now add up your points and determine your score.
Here's what your number means:

0 points: Well, you'd be naked!

12 points or under: Girlfriend, you need some accessories. It's time to run out and get some NOW!

12–14 points: Almost there, but not quite. Where can you add something? Do you need another bangle? How about another ring? Maybe you need to paint your nails.

14–16 points: Well done, my friend. You've got it goin' on!

Over 16 points: Too much, sister! Take some things off till you settle at 16.

What's Your Score?

What I'd love for you to do is to take this "test" every time you put on an outfit. It might seem a little obsessive or time consuming at first, but I promise you it will quickly become second nature. Once you've done this a few times, you'll know exactly what you need to look your best. And for those special occasions when you're not sure what or how much to put on, now you've got a system to follow. You won't look under-accessorized or overdone ever again.

Size Does Matter

Before I tell you how to summon the inner accessory queen in you to help you complete or even create your unique look, we have to begin by talking about size. Remember in the beginning of this book, I told you the perfect figure is a balanced one? To dress well is actually easier than it sounds, because it's all about proportion and understanding the size and shape of your body. It means that everything you put on should work in conjunction with how you're made.

This reminds me of my people-watching experiences in Miami. The one thing that always stuck out in my mind about these women's appearance was how well they were all accessorized. Not only did they have great pieces of jewelry and other accessories on, but the items were the right size. This begs the question, "Does size matter?" In this context, you bet it does!

Picture with me the following: A tall, heavyset woman enters your home. Her dress is printed with small flowers. Her earrings are tiny pearl clip-ons and she's wearing a necklace that has a small cross at the center. Her purse is the size of a postcard. Let me ask you, does this woman look bigger or smaller than she really is?

Now picture this. A skinny, petite woman enters your home. She is wearing a dress with large polka dots. She has on gigantic earrings and a large necklace and is carrying a purse that looks like the size of a big diaper bag. What do you think about this woman? Does she look bigger or smaller than she actually is?

I've never been an accessory girl, so this morning I was trying to count. I'm only up to 9. I guess I have some work to do!

Jean

The truth is, the taller woman looks bigger in her small prints and accessories, and the petite woman is overpowered by her large polka dots and huge accessories. The key is not to look bigger or smaller when you dress; the key is to look like you know what you're doing. When you choose accessories and prints that are proportionate to your frame size, your shape, and your height, then you will accomplish this.

What Kind of Girl Are You?

I've come up with a fun way to help you determine what size accessories, patterns, and handbags to buy. Every time my friend Cathy sees me, she always tells me I'm a rock star. What? Yes, a rock star! Even now, several years later, I still leave her presence feeling great, and yes, like a rock star, because she told me I look like one!

What about you? Have you ever thought of yourself as a rock star? How about a movie star? A glamour girl? You may find it a little uncomfortable to think of yourself in these labels, but trust me, it's really fun. This is how we are going to decide the best accessories for you.

Whenever I speak about this concept in my workshops, the audience goes nuts. The women get so excited they break out into, well, rock stars, movie stars, and glamour girls. Hey, if we can't have fun calling ourselves by cool names, who else is going to?

I've based this idea on three things: your height, your size, and your style. You look best and most polished when you dress in proportion to your shape and size. When you understand this, choosing accessories and handbags will be a cinch. The descriptions on the next page will show you whether you are a Rock Star, a Movie Star, or a Glamour Girl.

Find your category and then consider how you like to dress. What is your personal style? Are you someone who likes big things? The newest and trendiest styles? Would you rather get a root canal than be caught without makeup at the grocery store? Would you consider yourself pretty snappy when it comes to knowing how to put things

"Fashion is architecture. It is a matter of proportions."
Coco Chanel

What's Your Score?

together? If you answered yes to most of these questions, then feel free to move up a category. You can't move up two categories, but I give you permission to move up one.

If you are 5'8" and a size 10 or above, you are a Rock Star! For you, the bigger the accessories the better! Go for oversize handbags, large earrings, and big prints.

If you are 5'2" or under and are size 0–4, you are a Glamour Girl! Go small to near-medium in size, but never big or oversized. Don't overpower yourself. Smaller is better on you.

If you don't fit these two categories, then you are a fabulous Movie Star! Stay in the medium range of purses and accessories. Don't go too large and never too small. Midsize prints work best for you.

From left to right: a Glamour Girl, a Movie Star, and a Rock Star!

What You Really Need to Know

Now that you have determined what kind of woman you are, let me offer some basic tips about choosing accessories. Remember when I talked about keeping your point total to sixteen? The best thing to do to make accessories work for you is to divide these sixteen points into two categories: Basic (like clothes, hair, and makeup) and Extra (for accessories like jewelry, scarves, glasses, and so on). Here's an example:

Basic	Points	Extra	Points
Jeans	1	Wedding ring set	1
Blouse	1	Fun ring on right hand	1
Jacket	1	Watch	1
Nice haircut	1	Bangle	1
Makeup	1	Necklace	1
Nails done	1	Earrings	2
Shoes	2	Belt	1
TOTAL POINTS	8	TOTAL POINTS	8

As you can see, it's easy to come up with eight points in the Basic category because we rarely leave the house without clothes and shoes on, right? And most of us consider makeup a necessity, so reaching your eight points here is a breeze. Now all you have to think about is what falls into the other category, the Extra. Here comes the fun part!

Belts. They come in all sizes and materials — skinny, wide, medium, leather, plastic, fabric, woven weaves. Belts can add flavor and zest to many outfits. Try one on and see what you think. However, if you're a b body type, remember this particular accessory isn't very friendly to you.

Handbags. Here we have one of your most important accessories. Your handbag will tell more about your style than anything else you have on. Spend the most money you can on a quality bag without

> *Just last week I went out shopping and took your advice to shop for a new purse. I purchased a nice brown purse to match the color of my hair. It looks SO much better than my little black one I used to carry around. Thanks for the tip!*
>
> *Karen*

What's Your Score?

breaking your budget. If you can afford only one handbag, make sure to purchase one that is close to your hair color, as it will be the most complementary to your natural coloring. If you like to have more than one handbag, then feel free to experiment with color.

Pay close attention to the hardware on your handbags. If you wear mostly silver accessories, then choose a purse with silver hardware. If you wear mostly gold, then make sure it has gold hardware. The key to your style is carrying a handbag that balances your proportion. Rock Stars, be bold and go big! Movie Stars, stay more in the medium range. Glamour Girls, small to medium size is best for you. See the photo on page 71 so you can get a feel for the proportion of your handbag to your body.

Scarves. A scarf can make a fabulous addition to many outfits. I'd recommend you have several in multiple colors and prints. Scarves of today are not the same as yesteryear. The difference is the way you wear them. For an updated look, for instance, try draping a scarf around your neck and tie it in a loose knot just above or below the bustline. If you have only one scarf, make sure it's in one of your pop colors. Refer back to chapter 2 to remember what these are.

Necklaces. These beauties come in all lengths, shapes, and materials. Necklaces can add so much to an outfit because they draw attention to the center of your body, which makes you look thinner. If a necklace is shorter in length, it will also draw attention to your face. Please consider the size of your necklace to make certain it goes with your proportion. For example, you can wear an amazing turquoise necklace, but if it is too big for you, then it will "wear" you instead of you wearing it. Necklaces can be made of gold, silver, gold/silver mix, colorful beads, pearls, natural stones, and real gemstones. They can have a beautiful pendant as the focal point or have attractive accents all around it.

Bracelets. Bangles, charm bracelets, wooden ones, gold ones, silver ones, pearl ones. Wow! So many to choose from. Wearing an accessory on your wrist is a wonderful way to pull your look together. Try wearing a "buddy" with your watch by adding a simple bracelet on the same wrist as you wear your watch. I learned this tip from the Premier Designs Jewelry girls and I love the idea!

Pins. Pins are great if you like a romantic or vintage look. You can find fabulous ones in antique or second-hand stores, and they won't cost you a fortune. Add one at the knot in your scarf for a pretty look.

Earrings. Hoops, studs, small, large, too many to even list. Earrings are a must to finish any look. Make sure you wear the proper size for your scale. Not too small and not too big.

Shawls. Not everyone can wear shawls well, so make sure you're comfortable with this look or leave it alone. Shawls can add a dramatic flair to a jacket by being draped around the jacket. Tie it in a knot or add a pin to keep it in place.

Wraps. Pashmina wraps became popular several years ago and still are today. They come in all kinds of fabrics and many colors. Everyone should own one in their best color to keep warm on a cool summer night.

Rings. Costume jewelry rings or the real thing. It doesn't matter. Always add one to your finger. They look so chic.

Watches. A classic gold or silver watch adds polish to any outfit, but don't be afraid to go bold and bright for a more casual look.

Hosiery. Hosiery can add a fun look to any outfit and can also keep you warm when it's cold outside. Stay away from a suntan color. Those are outdated for sure. Choose tights that have a fun pattern or texture and wear them with skirts and dresses. Make sure you wear boots or closed-toe shoes with tights. If you must wear a nude color, match it to the inside of your forearm.

Sunglasses. Sunglasses are not only a necessity in our lives but can also make a big fashion statement. Since they come in all shapes and sizes, you'll want to try on lots of pairs before making a final decision. Feel free to break out of your usual fashion box with sunglasses and experiment a little. Try on oversized ones, aviators, pairs with cheetah prints. Have fun! When you read chapter 6, you'll find out the best frames for your face shape.

Shoes. This word is part of my love language because, oh, how I love me some shoes! Comfort or style, you might ask? For the most part, you don't have to choose, but some occasions generally call for one or the other. While loafers are comfy, for instance, you wouldn't wear them to a wedding. Nor would you wear high heels to an office picnic in the park. Every good girl needs some staple shoes in her wardrobe, including flats, heels, tennis shoes, and a smart pair of boots. But who wants only four pairs? I certainly don't. And I have the feeling you don't either!

Today I picked up this cheap, colorful set of wooden bead bracelets for less than four bucks. FOUR BUCKS! It's a group of colors and they go great with my general wardrobe AND my new lime-green leather handbag. :-) Now I'm off to search for a fun, colorful watch!

Jolynne

Who's Got Style? You Do!

Personal style trumps the trends every time.

I once heard someone say, "Personal style trumps the trends every time." I couldn't agree more. Unfortunately, a lot of women don't know what their personal style is, so they wear whatever they can find and end up with a mishmash of styles.

As a teenager, I knew I didn't dress like everyone else. I loved fashion (and still do, of course). I loved putting my personal touches on outfits. I loved the variety of colors and patterns I could play around with. But growing up in a small town in Ohio, many of my peers didn't feel as enthusiastic about style as I did. Because I felt pressure to look like everyone else, I downplayed my talent and dressed like the rest of my friends.

The minute my mother would announce a big shopping trip to the nearest city, my heart would start to beat a lot faster. It was time to

come out! As we prepared to leave, I put on a little more makeup and spent extra time on my hair. I pulled out the one pair of high platform patent leather pumps (I can still picture them today) I kept around for this special occasion. I put on my most fashionable jeans (whatever I had purchased the last time in the city) and waited as patiently as I could until we'd jump in the car and head to Cleveland. It was a teenage fashionista's dream.

I had my own style even as a young girl. I recently found my second grade class picture and noticed I was the only girl carrying a purse that matched my dress. What seven-year-old girl carries her purse to the class photo shoot? Me! As fifth graders, my friend Randi and I convinced each other to wear fashion's latest style called "knickers" to school. We were teased all morning long by our taunting friends who had never even seen such a fad before. Since Randi lived across the street from the elementary school, she immediately went home to change. I couldn't do a thing about it. I left the knickers on all day and endured another few hours of snickers.

As I entered adulthood, I kept on trying and wearing things

way before the trends dictated. Once I brought home a pair of snake-skin gladiator sandals much to my husband's dismay. He simply looked at me and shook his head. He knows better than to wonder if I'll wear them or why I bought them in the first place. My leather purse last season was bright orange and could have passed for a small suitcase. My turquoise necklaces and gigantic pearl bracelets are much bigger than the average woman would probably wear. You get the picture. I am what you would call a Style Fashionista.

Let's find your clothing personality. Are you a Style Fashionista, a Classic Modern, a Pure Natural, or a Creative Original? By now you know that if you sound anything like me — trying out the latest styles, stepping outside of the fashion box, and not being concerned with what others may think of you — you are a Style Fashionista. Read about some of the different women in my life and see where you fit in.

Style Fashionista

Meet Patti, my dear friend. Patti is a wife and the mother of two young children. She stays busy during the week by homeschooling her children and taking care of her home and church responsibilities, while also counseling married women part-time.

You will always find Patti wearing basic wardrobe pieces like tailored slacks, well-cut jackets, and smart blouses. She'll add colorful beads to many of her outfits, but for the most part, her accessories tend to be long silver chains with silver hoop earrings. She wears the prettiest scarves with her clothes and her beautiful, long mane of black hair is always carefully brushed into soft layers. She chooses stylish pumps and sandals, but if it's winter, she's never without a sleek pair of black boots. Even Patti's jeans are nice-fitting and always pressed.

Classic Modern

She'll usually add a nice white blouse with a bright colored jacket for flair. She also enjoys tailored sweaters and blazers. Patti adds an element of surprise to her wardrobe by always wearing one big ring. Patti likes classic pieces but modernizes her outfits with unique accessory choices like the ring or beads. Patti is Classic Modern.

My friend Barb owns a landscaping company. Barb moved to North Carolina from California with her husband and two boys, who are now both in high school. Even on the dressiest of days, you'll find Barb in a basic shift dress with pearls. You will never, and I mean never, find her wearing hose or tights of any kind. Barb likes to shop at Banana Republic, J. Jill, and Lands' End. Her wardrobe is full of khaki slacks and shorts, sleeveless and short sleeve polos, and she usually has on a pair of comfortable sandals or clogs. Barb wears her short blonde hair in an easy-to-care-for style, wears minimal makeup, and always has a bottle of sunblock nearby. Barb lives a casual lifestyle with casual clothes and has a casual, laid-back personality. Her clothes are mostly made of 100 percent fibers like cotton or silk. Barb is Pure Natural.

I'd like to introduce you to April. April is the women's ministry director at a megachurch and is the mother of three children under age thirteen. She keeps busy with church activities, and being an assistant to her musician husband. She is always smiling and is happy to help out anyone in need at a moment's notice. April usually wears dresses and skirts but is also known to wear great-fitting jeans or wide-leg pants. Her dresses are typically longer in length and may be solid in color or have a whimsical or artistic print on them. April always seems to find interesting jackets to wear with her skirts and pants. I don't think April wears makeup, but she does wear a little lipstick for special occasions. April wears her light brown hair in a length just at her shoulders and is usually wearing glasses. She wears antique earrings and a pretty watch along with her wedding ring. She also has lots of fun, colorful beads and bangles and unique shoes. April is what I like to call a Creative Original.

What about you? Which of these four styles has your name written all over it? You may be a combination, but I encourage you to choose one. This will help you build a beautiful wardrobe and learn to shop to suit your particular style. In chapter 8, I'll show you where you can find these kinds of styles.

A final word: Keep in mind your personal style when choosing accessories. If you are a Creative Original like April, look for one-of-a-kind pieces that show your creative flair. Your jewelry of choice may be inspired antique pieces or distinctive jewelry found at craft festivals. Shop for artsy handbags and shoes, and always be on the lookout for one-of-a-kind pieces to add to your wardrobe.

If you are a Pure Natural like Barb, then you will likely favor jewelry with turquoise and natural stones. Classic rings, necklaces, and bracelets in a silver or gold tone will suit you nicely. Carry a good leather handbag in a color close to your hair color since you most likely don't change purses for separate occasions.

If you are like Patti and are in the Classic Modern category, then you most likely love jewelry and won't have trouble reaching your sixteen points. You probably like bags from designers like Coach, Louis Vuitton,

Keep in mind your personal style when choosing accessories.

Pure Natural

Making the Count in the Accessory Game

and Chanel. However, if designer labels aren't in your budget, opt for classic bags of solid colors. You'll love pashmina scarves and wraps as they add the right amount of splash to your wardrobe.

And girlfriend, if you are a Style Fashionista, then anything goes as long as it's new, up-to-the-minute, and bold. Be brave (like I have to tell *you*!) and wear the new trends. Usually for you, the bigger the better, but remember if you are a Glamour Girl or Movie Star, don't go crazy. You can still make an impact without going huge. Find stylish necklaces and bangles to wear with the latest designer jeans you've got on.

Creative Original

What's Your Score?

But I Don't Know My Style Yet

Now I know some of you may be saying, "Wait a minute, Shari, I don't fit into any of these categories." Well, I've pulled out two extra categories where you might belong (at least for now).

After inventing the clothing personalities I just told you about, I was sitting in the airport on a long layover, passing the time people-watching. My assistant, Patti, was sitting next to me and we were discussing these clothing personalities and pointing out women whom we thought fit into each category. We had so much fun doing so.

But then we saw two women who stuck out from these groups. One was about twenty-eight years old and was wearing super low-rise jeans, a slim T-shirt, and ballet flats. The other woman was wearing baggy jeans, an ill-fitting T-shirt, and sensible shoes. After we noticed these two women, we started seeing more women who looked similar. It occurred to me then that way too many women don't even have a style, let alone fall into one of the four I described. So I created two more categories.

Trendy Twenties. This is a woman in her twenties who is stuck dressing like she is in college. At this age, many women haven't even thought about personal style. They've been wearing blue jeans and T-shirts for four years, and after graduating, are thrown into the workforce without a style clue. Their closet is crammed with dozens of jeans and tiny tops. Now I don't expect college graduates to drop what they've been wearing like a hot potato and become Style Fashionistas. There's something fresh and original about a girl in her twenties who can still shop in the Junior department, wear the latest trends, and not have to pay a fortune for them by finding them at discount stores like Target or Forever 21.

But herein lies the problem. How many of you reading this are dressing in the style of the Trendy Twenties but are no longer *in* your twenties? Are you still dressing like some of those gals I saw at the airport (and continue to see) but are in your thirties, forties, or even your fifties? Do you think you'll look younger by dressing

No matter what your age, consider that what you wear tells others what you think about yourself.

in clothes from the junior department? I hate to inform you, but you won't. Wearing overtly sexy clothes won't cut it either. No matter what your age, I hope you'll consider that what you wear tells others what you think about yourself. You will certainly get attention, but I'm afraid it's the wrong kind of attention.

If you still find yourself dressing as you did in your twenties, you are probably ready to start wearing clothes that represent your current place in life. It's time to add a few pieces to your wardrobe, like some classic blouses and sweaters and a few new accessories. In this chapter, you saw pictures of clothing for each of the style personalities, and I'd encourage you to take another look at them and see which category most appeals to you. Then try to begin dressing that way and start shopping in the recommended stores listed in the shopping guide.

I Ain't Got Style. This is a self-explanatory category and might be you. This kind of woman has been doing the same thing all these years — buying whatever is on sale, wearing black because she thinks it makes her look slimmer, and taking more care to dress her kids and husband than herself. She is the woman who looks in the mirror one

day and sees "frumpy" staring back at her. She has no style. If this is you, it's not too late to change. After all, after everything I've taught you in this book so far, how could I possibly leave you now?

In his book *How to Have Style*, Isaac Mizrahi instructs women who want to figure out their style to make an "inspiration board." He writes, "To help you discover your style, you need to know what inspires you — what colors you love, what images you are drawn to, which movies you watch over and over and love more each time."[2]

Isaac directs women to find visual inspiration and images by looking at advertisements, architecture, blogs, fashion and celebrity icons, flowers, postcards of places you've been, pottery and china, and scarves, to name a few. He suggests looking through magazines to find some things that inspire you, then cut them out and collect them on a corkboard. I want you to do this exact thing.

As you flip through magazines, pay attention to what catches your eye about particular advertisements or photographs. Are you inspired by new buildings with clean lines or old houses filled with collectibles? Maybe you like the look of a beach and the models with windblown hair who are wearing Ralph Lauren classic cotton dresses? Soon, you will see a pattern of influence which will point you in the direction of the clothing style (out of the four I've just described) that fits you best.

Perhaps you don't have time to make a style board. No problem! Look back at chapter 3 where you'll find the style personalities and photos identified with them. If you review these photos, you can decide which category appeals to you. You can also people watch and see what impresses you most about the different styles you see. I found much of my early inspiration in the world of fashion from watching the beautiful women in Miami. I admired how they wore accessories, how they tied their scarves, and even memorized the style of shoes they wore. Then I copied them. You can do the same. Look around and see what you like. Who dresses the way you wish you did? Sit down on a bench inside a busy mall, Starbucks in hand, and watch the people go by. Who looks sharp? Who looks sloppy? How would you like to dress? If you still don't know, don't worry; it may take some time, but I promise you'll eventually find your personal style.

> *"Fashion is not something that exists in dresses only. Fashion is in the sky, in the street, fashion has to do with ideas, the way we live, what is happening."*
>
> Coco Chanel

Now it's time to take a peek at what you are wearing underneath your clothes. I know this may be very unfamiliar territory for some of you, but wearing the right undergarments in the right way is very important. They can make you look balanced and even slimmer. Keep reading, girlfriend, I'm going to show you how.

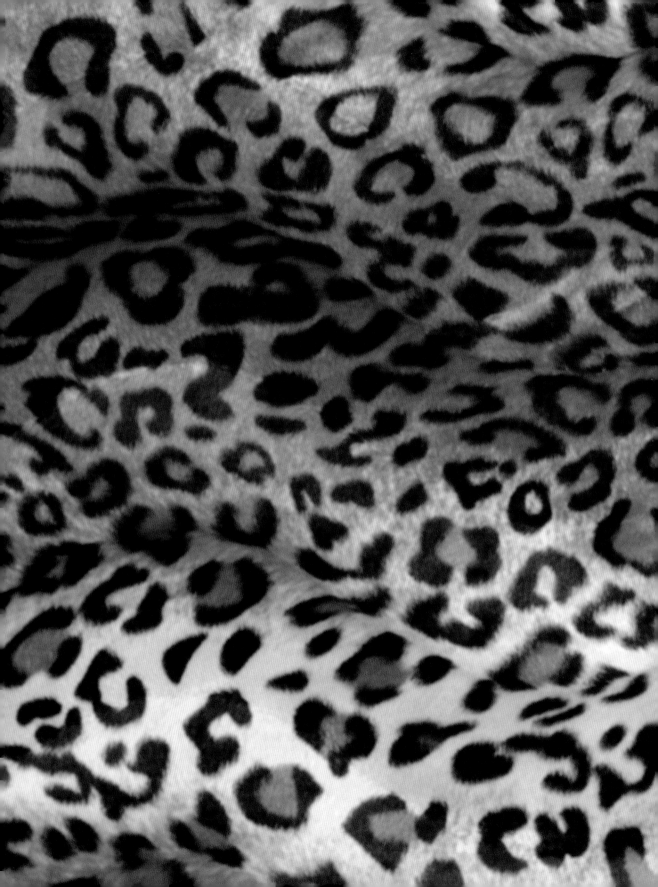

Whaddya Got Under There?

The Art of Undergarments

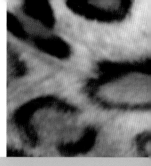
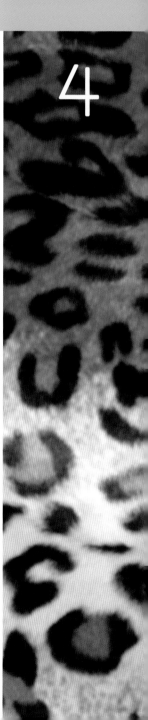

EIGHT OUT OF EVERY TEN WOMEN ARE WEARING THE WRONG size bra. Since a woman can typically wear up to six different bra sizes in her lifetime due to surgery, weight gain or loss, pregnancy, or by simply aging (can you imagine?), it's important to get a professional fitting at least once every twelve to eighteen months. You need to be sure you're still wearing the right one for you. If you've never been correctly fitted before, put it on your to-do list. It may not seem like a big deal, but if you really want to look your best, you have to have all your bases covered — and yes, that includes your "girls"!

Here is an email I received from a woman named Valerie that made me bust out laughing (pun intended):

> I persuaded my seventy-year-old mother to go with me to have a professional bra fitting. She reluctantly agreed, as she had never been fitted before and had always just purchased a bra on sale once every few years. When the bra specialist asked her to raise her arms so she could measure her "girls," my mom had to sit down she was giggling so hard! Once she composed herself and finally allowed the woman to measure her, she was then fitted for the proper bra. She couldn't believe she could look so perky after all these years and insisted on wearing the bra home! While we were standing at the cash register to pay, another customer approached the counter and my mother turned to her, pointed to the sales lady, and exclaimed, "She got my girls up! Look at them! Don't they look great?"

Don't Forget about the Girls!

A bra is the most important undergarment you can own. The very first time I was fitted for the right bra, it made a two-inch difference in where my "girls" were sitting. I felt like a new woman!

There are a few ways to get this accomplished. First, you can call your local department store to see if they have someone who is professionally trained to fit you. Better department stores and specialty shops offer this as a free service to their customers. (See? Even clothing stores understand that getting a proper bra fitting is well worth your time!)

A company I love called *Essential Bodywear* will actually send a qualified consultant to your home to provide you and your friends with a proper bra fitting. Imagine that. You can have a bra party! I've done this before and it's a lot of fun. Some Essential Bodywear specialists even carry inventory with them to the party, so you can buy bras and other undergarments on the spot. Other consultants allow you to place an order for delivery in a week or so.

Before I forget, when you schedule your appointment with a bra expert, you must find out if the person who will be fitting you has had proper training. Don't even bother getting fitted by someone who hasn't (you might as well keep wearing your old bra).

Second, I'm going to give you a do-it-yourself technique. I know there are plenty of you women who have already decided that you'd rather jump in a lake than have someone else take your measurements. Not a problem! I'll share some know-how so you can do this in the privacy of your own home. All this takes is two easy steps. You'll need a measuring tape, so be sure to have one handy.

Step 1: Measure at the top of your breasts while pulling the tape under your armpits and around your back. Pull the tape as tight as possible. (See picture for example.) Write down the measurement number.

Step 2: Take the tape and measure at the fullest part of your bustline and hold the tape loosely. Write that measurement down.

STEP 1

The first measurement relates to your band size. The second measurement relates to your cup size. You need to count the difference in inches between the two numbers to get your cup size as follows:

The first inch equals an A cup
The second inch equals a B cup
The third inch equals a C cup
The fourth inch equals a D cup
And so on …

STEP 2

Here's an example. Let's say the first measurement is a 34 and the second measurement is a 38. There is a four inch difference between those two numbers, so you would wear a 34 D bra.

This may not be the most foolproof method of measuring, but if it's the best you can do, at least it's a start. I do wish you'd go to a professional, though, or let one come to you. The greatest mistake women make is they buy bras for comfort instead of support. And I'm afraid if left to your own measuring, you might end up making the same mistake.

I'm so excited to tell you I got fitted for a new bra! When I arrived home my husband asked, "What did you do? You look ten years younger!" I told her I got a new bra. He looked me up and down and said, "Oh my goodness, it really did make a difference! You look amazing, honey."

Wilene

Proper measuring can make a world of difference. I promise you'll look so much better in your clothes. If it's too intimidating for you to go to a store alone, bring your best friend for support. Hey, she might need a fitting too.

How many bras should you own? Experts tell us you should have at least three bras in your undergarment wardrobe: the one you are wearing, one in the laundry basket, and one in your drawer waiting to be worn. Three bras, you might ask? Well, yes. When you wear a bra two days in a row, you run the risk of the elastic getting stretched out. When it gets a day to rest, it will actually regain its shape and will last so much longer.

Tips & Tricks

Here are a few tips on bras you might like to know:

- A flesh tone is the best color bra to have. You may then add other colors as you wish.
- Did you know you should wear a bra to bed? This helps your girls stay firm so they don't lose their elasticity.
- Hand wash your bras for the best possible care. If this is totally out of the question, then throw them into a lingerie bag with all the bra clasps done up and make sure the bag is closed tightly. To dry, lay your bra flat, cup side up.
- Summer tops and dresses may require a strapless bra, so have one handy for those pieces.
- If you've had a mastectomy, many pretty bras will fit you, but ask your bra specialist to show you how to insert gel pads for an even and smooth look.
- Wear a sports bra when exercising to hold your girls in place.

- If you have dark nipples and it seems nothing you do keeps them from showing through your clothes, get some Gel Petals. These look like small Band-Aids and fit directly over your nipples. Each petal gives you approximately twenty-five wears and can be purchased in most department stores.

- When you try on a new bra, walk in place in front of a mirror. Make sure your girls are not bouncing up and down as you walk.

- Your girls should sit halfway between your elbow and the top of your shoulder. If you're like most women, yours are probably hanging a little too low.

- If you have trouble with your bra straps slipping off your shoulders, you can buy a bra clip for exactly this purpose. You can also use a bra clip to hold back the straps and hide them when wearing clothes that would otherwise require a strapless bra.

> *You'll be happy to know that the only bra store in our neck of the woods, "Girlfriends," was so busy on Saturday that there was an HOUR WAIT to be fitted for a bra. Probably all those Hearts at Home gals who went to your seminar!*
>
> *Michelle*

Q: **How do I find a bra when my breasts seem to be different sizes?**

A: There is an easy solution for this. You can purchase silicone inserts to slip inside the bra cup of the smaller breast. Since these feel much like breast tissue, they are not noticeable under your clothes and mold right to your bra. Push-up bras are another option. They come with removable inserts, also known as cookies, and you can place the cookie inside the cup of the smaller breast to balance your figure.

Q: **Should I buy matching bras and panties?**

A: There was a time in my life when I only wore bras and panties that matched exactly. I've found, though, that with the price of lingerie these days, this seems to be a bit excessive. My suggestion is to buy neutrals. When wearing a black lace bra, pair it with black panties, white with white, and so on. If you prefer colorful prints for your panties, then wear them with the most prominent neutral color you find in the bra. For example, if your bra is nude in color, wear the printed panties with the nude background. This way you can still match without it being exact.

Q: **I have spillage. What should I do?**

A: Make sure your bra has good coverage, as you may be in the wrong style bra for you. The most common help for this problem, however, is to go up a cup size.

Q: **My band rides up in the back. Help!**

A: When standing in front of a mirror, your band should be even all the way around your chest. If it is not, then try going up a cup size or down a band size. Most likely, you need a new bra and a professional fitting.

Q: My straps won't stay on my shoulders. Is there a solution for this?

A: Yes, there is. If you're sure your bra is the correct size for you, try bra clips. This simple accessory will have your bra straps staying up in no time. These attach your straps together in the back and work beautifully. You can pick up a set for under $10 in most lingerie departments. You also can try a racerback-style bra.

Q: Ouch! My straps dig into my shoulders!

A: There are pads you can purchase in the bra and panties department that you can place under your straps if you're sure you are wearing the correct bra; however, most likely, your straps are working too hard and you need to get a new bra. This happens when your band size or cup size is wrong. Consider purchasing a bra that has padded shoulder straps.

Q: My cups look like they're "dimpling." What's that all about?

A: It's time to go down a cup size. Did you lose some weight?

Q: I have the dreaded "back fat." Please help!

A: Try Bra-llelujah by Spanx. It virtually eliminates back fat because of the material it is made of (hosiery material) and is wide enough to smooth the back. It has a front clip closure. Also, back fat typically happens when the band size is too loose. When the band size is corrected, this will reduce the appearance of back fat.

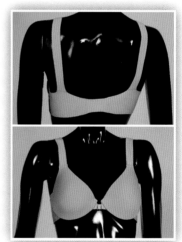

The Bra-llelujah by Spanx

Q: Help! I'm an AA. What bras work best for me?

A: There are beautiful options for small-chested women. You can wear very pretty bras that will enhance your shape by trying one of these: Wacoal Petite, Jasmine Ginger, or Lula Lu. Also, don't let "petite" confuse you either. Wacoal Petite is referencing your bust size, not your height.

Panties, Panties & More Panties

If you have ever perused the racks of underwear in department stores or other shops, you know there is a plethora of different styles. So what to choose? Your decision can be mostly guided by comfort (and what doesn't stick out for the world to see, of course). Here are the most popular models:

Brief. This full coverage underwear comes in extended sizes and is great for the plus size gal or any size woman who wants excellent coverage. It offers a comfortable waistband, tummy coverage, and natural fit of the leg openings, and there is no riding up. Recommended brands: Jockey, Hanes, Gilligan & O'Malley, Bali.

Thong. This is a thin and lightweight underwear, perfect for hiding panty lines. Recommended brands: Calvin Klein, B.Tempt'd, Maidenform, BCBGeneration.

Bikini. This is a basic style for those who want little coverage and maximum comfort. Recommended brands: Hanes, Calvin Klein, B.Tempt'd, Maidenform, Gilligan & O'Malley.

Hi-Cut Brief or ***French Cut.*** These panties provide great tummy coverage and sport the look of a bikini. Recommended brands: Jockey, Vanity Fair, Wacoal, Bali.

Boy Short. This practical option does not show panty lines and fits most body types. There is no "riding up" and it is very comfortable. Buy a size larger for this and most all underwear styles to prevent riding up and too tight panties. Recommended brands: Calvin Klein, Tommy Hilfiger, Fruit of the Loom, DKNY.

Shape It, Girlfriend, Shape It!

No woman's undergarment wardrobe is complete without a little (or a lot) of shapewear. Hey, even the size 2 celebrities wear this miracle stuff to keep them looking firmed and toned! If they can do it, why can't we?

I love the way my friend Rhonda Barrera, manager of the lingerie department at Dillard's, explained it. She said the way she looks at it, you can either spend $5,000 for plastic surgery to suck away all your extra fluff, or you can spend $85 on a good shaper and you'll get the same visual results! I think I'd rather have the extra money to spend on a few new clothes or a trip to Hawaii! How about you?

While none of us have the perfect body, we do have options on how we look in our clothes. We can either look smoothed out, squished out, or sucked in.

I'm not suggesting you wear a shaper (or as I like to call it, a "sucky-in-thingy") with all your clothes, though I know some women who do. Shapers, at least in my opinion, are for those special clothing items that need a little extra help in making you look a little less fluffy. It's for those clothes where your muffin top won't go away or for that dress or slacks, that no matter what you do, you can still see bumps and bulges underneath. A shaper is not something you'll probably wear with jeans and a sweatshirt, but once you see how good you look in your clothes with one on, you might want to wear it with everything. This is totally up to you.

> I am a FIRM believer in "sucker-inners." I wear them especially for special events where I wouldn't see those people for another year. At least I am going to look good for that one night, right? There is nothing like a confidence booster when you have all your fat rolls firmly tucked away in one place!
>
> *Ashley*

Here's a rundown on the types of shapers that are available:

Top Support. This is like a cami that offers very firm support. It has a built-in bra but can also be worn over your regular bra. This will smooth your upper midriff and muffin top. Great for b and o body types.

Panty Support. This panty is for tummy and butt support. It holds in your tummy and lifts your butt. It actually lifts and smoothes your bottom to make you look like a perky teenager again! Recommended for b body types.

Mid-Thigh. This is for the body type who has an issue with the hip and thigh areas. This shaper firms the tummy, butt, and hip sections. Recommended for d body types or someone who is a combination of b and d. o body types will love this too.

Full Body. This is for everything — the tummy, butt, hips, and thighs. It offers complete body support to firm it all up and suck it

Top support

Panty support

Mid-thigh

Full body

Whaddya Got Under There?

all in. This shaper starts just below the bustline and goes to the knee. Great for anyone who desires all over support.

There are several different types of body shapers available, but my favorite is made by Spanx. You can find these styles in the better department store. Prices range between $50 and $85. This may seem like a lot of money, but the comfort, fit, and quality is money well spent. And remember, it's much cheaper than surgery! Essential Bodywear has their own shaper which is also excellent. In fact, I own one and like it a lot. It costs about $60.

For those of you who don't want to spend that much but still want to try out a shaper, Target carries Sarah Blakely's Bodyshaping Collection called Assets. Sarah Blakely is the inventor of Spanx and her line in Target costs in the $15 – $25 range. You might even catch them on sale every now and then. I have a pair of hers that holds my tummy in and ends just below my knees. I wear them with my slacks and it helps my legs to appear bump-free.

I wear shapers and I LOVE them! I have a black pair and a white pair. They take away the ring around the middle and make my baby belly almost invisible. Shapers also add a slimming effect to all my outfits.

Tamal

At the time I was writing this book, it was early spring. As you can imagine, the clothing stores had already put out a wide selection of everyone's favorite piece of clothing. That's right, bathing suits! I think I can hear you groaning and protesting, but you can put a stop to your tantrum now. I'm going to show you how to get the best swimsuit for you without the pain and tears.

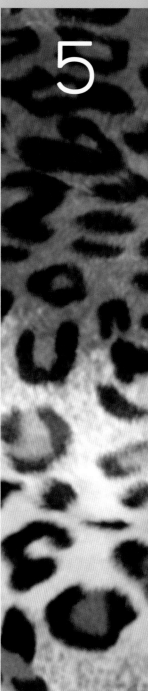

Survival of the Smartest:
How to Divide and Conquer Swimwear

5

YOU WALK INTO A DEPARTMENT STORE, MAYBE HOPING TO BUY A new pair of sandals or a stylish peasant blouse or a new lipstick. Just as your shoes touch down on the linoleum floor after you walk through the revolving doors, you see *them* in all their glory.

There are many of them. In a multitude of colors. Some the size of postage stamps. Some in the shape of burlap sacks. They beckon to you because they know *you* know it's time. Memorial Day is around the corner, after all. Pools and beaches will be open. Soon, you will need to don a swimsuit. "I'm not ready!" you yell to yourself. But, girlfriend, summer has arrived. And the swimsuit you wore last summer, the one in the unflattering color that did nothing to accentuate the gorgeous features on your body, needs to be tossed in the trash.

It's time to approach the swimsuit department with confidence, not apprehension. And maybe even with a twinge of excitement. Imagine that! It's time to find out how to camouflage your trouble spots without overtly looking like you are trying to hide them. It's time to find out what style swimsuit is best suited for your body. It's time to gain some insight into how to look even more beautiful while strolling on the beach or frolicking with the kids in the community pool.

You may have initially been attracted to this book solely because of this chapter. If you're like most women, the thought of swimsuit season is a freakish nightmare. There is no need to be afraid; help is on the way! Surviving the swimsuit season takes raw courage, but as you have learned about your body and how to dress it with your everyday wardrobe, you can do the same with your swimsuit.

Give Yourself a Break!

Before you embark on the task of finding the perfect swimsuit for you, you need to be truthful with yourself when it comes to your body. No one has a perfect body. Not you, not me. But your body is still beautiful, so embrace it. Accept it. Learn to love it.

Unless you are a teenager (and even then it might not be the case), no one has a perfectly toned, firmed, and smooth body without some bulges or bumps. We do not live in Hollywood where we have our plastic surgeon's phone number on speed dial. We do not walk out of our houses after being airbrushed.

No body is perfect. I cannot stress this enough. I even know of some size 2 women who have certain body parts they are not thrilled with. Sometimes even exercise or following the right diet perfectly can't make you look exactly the way you want, so don't be so hard on yourself.

Now, we need to be realistic. When you're in your bathing suit, things show. Understand that I can get you looking pretty good in a swimsuit, but I can't tone your bumps and bulges. Know that the goal in purchasing the perfect swimsuit is to help you look the best you possibly can in swim attire; it's not to hide all your flaws. Quite frankly, that's not going to happen. But be encouraged. Have faith that you can look pretty darn good in a swimsuit!

When I buy a bathing suit, one test I always do is bend over and look in the mirror, at both the front and the back. I spend so much time standing in the baby pool, bending over my child, I figure I better check out all views of myself before I get out there for the world to see. It doesn't matter how good my suit looks when I'm standing up straight. If anything spills out of the front or slips out of the back when I'm assuming the "mommy pose" at the pool, then I'm in big trouble!

Kathryn

Survival of the Smartest:

Getting Back to the Basics

Our starting point is your body type and its specific challenge and asset areas. Are you a b, o, d, or x? Flip through chapter 1 again if you need a refresher course.

The thing that is unique about searching for a new swimsuit is that we can't look at the body as a whole. Instead, we have to look at our body in sections. Therefore, I will describe the different areas on your body, and you will be guided to shop accordingly. For example, if you have a full bust, you are probably an o body type, but you might also be busty as a b, d, or x.

Remember, the goal is to take the attention away from your challenge areas, to keep in balance, and to look proportionate. The same is true when choosing swimwear. Different body types look better in particular suits. You know the saying, "A picture is worth a thousand words?" There will be pictures here to show you what I mean.

This brings to mind what it took to get photos in this chapter. I wanted real women for models in my book, not professionals. So when I began looking for women to model the swimwear, I went straight to my friends. Let me tell you what, this was no easy task. I begged and I pleaded. I bribed them with personal shopping services, lunch, dinner, my firstborn, you name it. None of them took the bait. They all looked right into my eyes and without hesitation said, "N-O! NO!"

After more begging and pleading from me and putting on my saddest, puppy-dog face, they all finally said yes! Under one condition. They threatened that if I showed their faces, they wouldn't be my friends anymore. This is why you see them all wearing these gorgeous hats!

Time for Some Self-Assessing

Before heading to the nearest mall, there are a few things you need to do at home first.

Start by putting on your bathing suit from last year, and then stand in front of a full-length mirror. (If you haven't bought a full-length mirror yet, you can get one at a local Target or Walmart for under $10.)

Inspect yourself from all angles. Please don't skip doing this. You may be thinking that you don't have to try on last year's suit, that you'd rather forget what you looked like in it, but trust me, it's important to do so. It's not until you have a true picture of yourself in a swimsuit that the rest of this chapter will make sense.

When you look at yourself full on, how do you think this bathing suit looks? Does it conceal your fluffiest parts? Stand sideways and check out that view. If you gain your weight in your tummy (b), does your suit hold you in as well as it could? You might even be an o, d, or x and have put on extra weight in your stomach area and want to camouflage that part. Now don't forget to check out the back view. Does your suit fully cover your bottom or do you see some fluffiness hanging out?

If you are a hip and thigh girl (d), what kind of leg-eye (this is the term for the opening in the leg) does last year's suit have? Where does it stop on your thigh? Is it cut high on your leg or not? Is it skirted? Do you like the way it looks?

How about your chest area? If you have a large bust, is your suit flattering to you, in your opinion? Does it make you look droopy? Is there spillage? Is your bust lined up where it is supposed to be, between your elbows and your shoulders?

Do you like the color of your suit? Does it flatter you? Wearing a color that helps you look vibrant is crucial to a swimsuit. Did you pick out last year's suit in a color that makes your complexion appear lively? Remember, the right color will actually help to slim you, so keep this in mind when shopping for your new swimsuit. When you need to start looking for one, visit your local department stores or swimsuit specialty shops and look for the brands I mention.

Assessing yourself in your bathing suit will help you approach purchasing this year's suit with a fresh perspective. Don't be nervous when you do this. And don't only look at your flaws and the body parts you want to hide better. Find some positive things about your body and point those out as well. Perhaps your suit shows off your athletic legs, your curvy waist, or your strong shoulders. Don't use this self-assessment task to judge your body or berate yourself. Look in the mirror and remind yourself how cute you are!

For you online shoppers, follow the advice for your specific body type to narrow down what you want in a swimsuit.

Ground Rules

Here are a few general rules to keep in mind as we get started:

1. Plan ahead what stores you are going to visit on your shopping outing. Pick one or two stores that you know have a good selection of swimwear, and stick to these for the day. Too many store choices may cause confusion and frustration.

2. You will most likely go up one size for a swimsuit. If you wear a size 10 in your clothes, you'll probably wear a 12 for your bathing suit. This is normal. Don't freak out. Cut the tag out if you want to forget what size your suit is. The most important thing is to look GOOD in your swimsuit, not squeeze into it like a stuffed sausage.

3. Take last year's suit with you so you can compare.

4. Wear teeny-weeny underwear for this shopping experience, as you will have to keep your panties on when trying on suits. Don't be caught with your granny panties on! For those of you who don't wear panties (you know who you are), don't forget to wear a pair that day.

Don't use this self-assessment task to judge your body or berate yourself.

5. If you have kids, leave them at home. This is not the place to hear them "oohing" and "ahhing" about how good Mommy looks in a swimsuit. Don't trust their judgment. And you don't need the added stress of hearing them say, "Are we going yet?" "I have to pee." "I'm hungry!"

6. If you have a good friend who also needs a suit, consider inviting her along. But let me caution you about something. If your best friend is a size 6 and you are a size 16, you might want to take a friend who is closer in size to you. The reason I say this is because women tend to have "show and tell" in the dressing room. When you see your smaller-size friend looking all cute in her size 6 swimsuit, you may get depressed with how you look. Just something to think about.

Finding a great swimsuit is not going to happen if you are in a hurry.

7. If your skin is more on the milky-white side, you might want to apply a self-tanner before you head out shopping. I laughed so hard when my friend Dawn told me that tan fat looks much better than white fat. Oh dear! But this is up to you. Your skin, whatever color, is still beautiful!

8. Do NOT try on swimsuits with socks or shoes. Get a pedicure and show off those cute feet.

9. Make sure you give yourself plenty of time to shop. Don't rush this process. Finding a great swimsuit is not going to happen if you are in a hurry. Never shop on impulse.

10. Finally, take this book with you. Mark up this chapter where applicable to your body type, and then bring it along. This is serious business, girlfriend.

Survival of the Smartest:

Help for Your Challenge Areas

I have done extensive research on swimwear, and there is so much information out there, even I started to get confused. So I'm keeping this simple for you. As I've mentioned before, I'm breaking up my recommendations based on specific sections of your body, common trouble spots for most women. Please get out a highlighter or pen and start marking up each area that applies to your body. This will help you formulate a plan for getting the perfect swimsuit. (You may read some terms you are unfamiliar with, so check out the mini glossary at the end of this chapter to help you on your way.)

Let me start with some general advice on the basic types of swimwear. A one-piece swimsuit is the most flattering style for every body, no matter your shape or size. It is also the most common type of bathing suit out there. Tankinis are also very popular and give the illusion of a one-piece even though this style is designed as a two-piece. Whether you choose a one-piece suit or a two-piece tankini, the look will be the same.

Bikinis are cute, but not very flattering on most body types. Truthfully, many aren't that modest either. As Christian women, we have a responsibility to the guys around us not to trip them up. I'm sure there are a few readers out there who think Christian women shouldn't even be wearing swimsuits, but let's get real. If you are hanging out on a beach or at a pool, what are you going to wear? A bathrobe? A jogging suit? Of course not. Bathing suits are a part of life. The key is to find one that's both modest and stylish.

Do you want to conceal your middle area? (b, o, d, x)

No matter your shape or size, if you want to conceal your middle area, look for a suit made with extra spandex or Lycra. This is an important rule for anyone who has a little more in the tummy, upper or lower midriff, or a muffin top. Even though most of what I described falls under the b body type, you may be an x and need to conceal a

As Christian women, we have a responsibility to the guys around us not to trip them up.

little belly or muffin top. Maybe you're an o who has a combination body type. Perhaps you're a d who has gained a little more weight in your tummy and you want to hide it a bit.

Ask the salesclerk to show you some brands like Magicsuit, SPANX, or the famous Miraclesuit. These swimsuits don't come cheap but are well worth the extra money. For example, the Miraclesuit is made with an innovative new fabric called Miratex which has three times as much spandex as the average swimwear fabric. Their promise is to make you look ten pounds lighter in ten seconds. And let me tell you, it does! Keep on the lookout for other brands that promise extra slimming power, because they really will make a difference on your body.

One last thing: patterns make your tummy look flatter. Don't be shy when it comes to deciding whether or not a pattern will work for you. Because it will.

Patterns make your tummy look flatter.

Do you have no waist? (b, o)

Look for a style that will create an illusion of a waist. Try a swimsuit that has a crossover or shirred middle area (if you don't know what these words mean, check out the mini glossary at the end of this chapter). A suit that draws the attention to the center of your body is the key. Side shirring is a beautiful look for you.

Do you have a small bust? (d, b, x)

As a small-busted woman, support isn't an issue for you, so you have more options than someone who has a larger bust. The idea is to make your top appear balanced with your hips, so look for swimsuits that have interesting details on the top. Choose decorative rings, ruffles, gathers, patterns, prints, contrasting colors (like pink and orange together), or ruching. Stay away from solid colors, dark colors, and plain tops. You may also want to look for a top with built-in padding.

Do you have a large bust? (**o**, **b**, **x**)

As a woman with a full bustline, support is key. You must always opt for a swimsuit that has a built-in bra with an underwire. While paying attention to support and coverage, look for suits with prints, patterns, darker colors, high cut armholes, and V-necks. These all help minimize your fuller bustline.

Do you want to hide your hips? (**d**)

The problem with swimsuits of yesteryear is they've exposed your hips and left them wide out in the open. Not anymore! Seek out suits that have a skirted bottom or a high-cut leg. The new swim skirts of today are fashionable and won't have you looking like you're wearing a dress at the pool. These skirted suits come in different lengths, from as short as eight inches to as long as fourteen inches. Make sure your swim bottom is longer than the fullest part of your leg. Don't let it stop right where your fullest part starts, otherwise you defeat the purpose of camouflaging this area.

If you don't like a skirted suit, get a swimsuit with a high-cut leg, then add a cute wrap to wear so you'll feel more comfortable. Buy one that coordinates with your suit. Draw attention to the top portion of your body, away from your bottom half, by wearing a suit with pretty detailing up top. Do not wear a halter neck top. Look for straps that sit wide on your shoulders to balance your hips.

Great suit option for a d body type

Are you straight and narrow? (b, x)

Add a few curves with strategically placed patterns, gathers, or cut-outs. Buy suits that have designs and patterns centered in the middle of the suit to create the illusion of a curvy figure.

Do you have a long body? (any body type)

Look for styles that have a lower neckline and a low leg-eye as this will reduce the length of your body. Skirted suits are also a good option for you. Look for suits that have bust seams. Avoid vertical designs or stripes at all costs.

Do you have a short torso or legs? (any body type)

Opt for vertical stripes and prints to elongate your body. High cut leg-eyes will lengthen your legs.

A great suit for a plus size

Are you a plus size gal? (any body type)

Don't be afraid of bold prints. You'll want to look for a suit that has extra Lycra, such as the Miraclesuit described before. Make sure your suit has good comfort and support. It's important to spend a little more money on your swimsuit, as quality is important and will help you appear thinner because of minimizing fabric. Your suit should have 15 – 20 percent Lycra or spandex. A couple of brands to try are Delta Burke and Swim 365.

Do you have heavy arms?

Wear a suit that shifts attention to the neckline by choosing a bathing suit that has lots of detail, decorations, or a print in the center part of the suit. You also will want to purchase a cover-up the same color of the swimsuit with sheer arms, to help conceal these parts when you're not swimming or sunbathing.

Survival of the Smartest:

Extra, Extra, Extra . . .
Read More Helpful Tips!

If you have large breasts but are petite, buy a swimsuit made with good, strong straps. Lightweight or flimsy straps will not support your heavy breasts, and you will look out of proportion. You'll also need a good underwire bra built into your suit.

If you have a double chin or a short neck, go for a suit with a V-neck shape or a suit without shoulder straps. Stay away from high neck cuts.

Your swimsuit should be long enough to stay put when you walk or run. It will ride up if it is not long enough on your body. Sit, bend over, twist, turn, stretch, walk, and run in place with your suit on to make sure it stays where it's supposed to. If your suit rides up or seems to cut into your body, it is either the wrong style for you or the wrong size.

Additional tips about styling for your specific body type:

Camouflage your tummy by wearing a suit with strong minimizing fabric. Solids are okay as long as they have some shirring on the fabric, but patterns are best. Find suits with curvy detailing like trim, piping, buttons, or princess seams. Tankinis are super for you, especially those that have a bit of flair to the top so they don't cling to your stomach. Halter tops are very flattering for your body type.

A flattering suit for a b body type

An **o** body type looks great in this swimsuit

You must have strong bra support. A suit like the Miraclesuit or Longitude is best. Patterns and solid colors with shirring or details are most suitable for you, and the support from a minimizing suit will hold you in all over.

Stay away from halter-type tops and choose wide shoulder straps to give the appearance of balance for your hips. If you have a small chest, as most d's do, you'll want to add bulk to your top area by adding horizontal stripes or prints. Padding will add a cup size. Skirted suits look super on you, as long as they don't hit at the exact spot where the fullest part of your thigh is.

Another great suit option for a **d** body type

Girl, you've got it so good! You can wear most any type suit, but please pay attention to the other body types if you have a tendency to gain a little weight and be out of balance. Know your challenges and assets and buy a swimsuit accordingly.

✑

With all this great information at your fingertips, take some time and make some notes about what you need in the perfect swimsuit. This will help you when you go shopping. Perhaps you need a suit with a built-in bra, one made out of spandex or Lycra, or one with a high-cut leg. Write down the top five qualities of a bathing suit that will make your shape look great!

Don't forget that one of your top priorities is to choose a swimsuit in a color that is flattering to you. If you prefer a swimsuit in a dark color, then choose wisely. If black isn't for you, then select a deep hue, like chocolate. Your cover-ups should be in colors that will bring you to life. Don't skip this important detail!

A swimsuit for an X body type

1. _____

2. _____

3. _____

4. _____

5. _____

Don't Forget About Accessories

No swimsuit would be complete without something to cover it up while you are going to and from the beach or pool. Since swimwear is a part of your wardrobe, consider a cover-up an important addition. I know many women who throw on shorts and a T-shirt with their bathing suit, but you will feel so much prettier in a special cover-up designed for your activities in the sun.

Many swim manufacturers design cover-ups to coordinate with the different styles of swimwear, so you can be sure to find one in the same print or color of your suit. Whether you are buying your suit at a department, specialty, or discount store, you'll find cover-ups in a wide range. Here are some of them:

Sarong: This is a long, wide scarf that looks like a shawl. When it is lying flat, it looks like a large triangle or square. It is also called a pareo. You can wear this as a hip scarf and tie it at the side in a knot, or wear this above the bustline tied into a knot.

Tunic: A tunic is a like a large top that is loosely fitted to be worn on your upper body. They range in lengths, so find one long enough to cover the parts of your body you want covered. These can be pulled over your head or can have buttons or zippers. You will find these in many fabrics, such as terry cloth and sheer nylon.

Dress: You can find loose, pretty, flowing dresses to be worn as swimsuit cover-ups. These come in florals, prints, and solids.

Swim Cover-Up Shorts: If you have great legs, this is a good option for you. Swim shorts are typically shorter in length, but many manu-

---

Ahhh, swimsuit season! What about cover-ups and accessories?
I never know what to wear over my suit when I'm headed to the pool.
I don't want to look like I'm trying too hard, but I don't want to look like I'm wearing my bathrobe either!

Beth

Survival of the Smartest:

facturers make these the same color as their swimsuits to create a very coordinated look.

Palazzo Pants: These wide-leg pants look extra special with bathing suits and add a dressier flair to your suit. They look great when paired with your swimsuit as the top. Wear with a straw hat at a pool party and you'll be the most stylish one there.

Long T-shirt Cover-up: These are very popular at family vacation spots and usually have a printed motif on the front like seashells, fish, or the name of the beach. Even though these are popular and will cover you up, they are the most casual and are not very figure flattering.

A word about cover-ups and accessories. Remember when we discussed whether you are a Style Fashionista, Classic Modern, Pure Natural, or Creative Original? I want to encourage you to bring your unique style into your world of swimwear. If you love glitz and glamour, get a cover-up with sequins. If you're more original, find a wrap with wonderful details that represents who you are. Pure Naturals, find a long linen blouse that could work as a great cover-up. And for you Classic Modern gals, a pareo would be a natural choice.

The same principle applies to your sunglasses and shoes. Bring forth your style with those items too! Now, I'm not going to suggest you go all out and wear your 16 points to the beach, but I am going to recommend a few items for you to have in your beach wardrobe. Honestly, you'll probably get to 14 points if you do it right! A swimwear wardrobe should consist of:

- Flattering swimsuit
- Coordinating cover-up
- Sunglasses
- Straw hat or trendy baseball cap for sun coverage
- Summery sandals, canvas, or mesh shoes
- Fun beach bag
- Simple earrings
- Painted toes
- Sunblock
- Beach towel

Swimsuit Mini Glossary

Tops

Bandeau Style. A strapless style suit that gathers in the middle front at the bustline. These usually come with attachable straps.

Halter Style. Halter style swimsuits have straps that tie around your neck. This adds instant lift to your bustline. Do not wear if you have narrow shoulders. This is particularly a no-no for d body types, unless your shoulders are not narrow.

Racerback Style. A one-piece swimsuit with a T-shaped back and strong top support. A popular style for competitive swimwear. Wonderful for full-busted women because it has excellent support.

Straight Style. This suit has straps that go straight over the shoulders and attach to the back of the suit on the back. It is also called a wide-strap top.

Bottoms

Bikini. Smallest coverage bottom.

Hipster. Sits lower on the hips for full seat coverage. Great for the shorter torso.

High-waist. A classic style that sits about 1" below the belly button. Higher cut on leg. Great when paired with a tankini.

Mid-waist. Moderate coverage and sits about 2" below the belly button with a slightly lower leg-eye.

Survival of the Smartest:

Swimsuit Styles

Boy Leg Suit. The coverage of this suit extends to the upper thighs and is great for d body types or those who might want to hide a little jiggle. Offers great support.

Maillot. Classic one-piece suit.

Skirted Swimsuit. This suit looks like the classic maillot, but has a skirted bottom instead of the regular leg openings.

Surplice Style. This suit minimizes the tummy by acting as a wrap around the mid section by drawing the attention elsewhere. It drapes nicely over the tummy and is a great camouflager.

Swim Dress. Looks just like a fitted dress that you can wear in the pool! This suit provides the most coverage.

Tankini. "Meet and Greet" suit. Two-piece suit where the top part meets the bottom part. There are tankinis that don't meet and greet, however, and a portion of the tummy shows.

Additional Terms

Leg-Eye. Refers to the leg opening.

Ruching. Fabric that is gathered, usually on the tops of swimsuits so a bust can appear larger. Sometimes used at the sides of swimsuits to give the appearance of a curvy body.

Shirring. A sheer layer of fabric that doubles over the swimsuit, so an area of the body can appear slimmer. It creates an illusion of a flatter area. Many swimsuits have shirring over the belly area.

See, that wasn't so bad, was it? I hope you're not afraid of swimsuits anymore! Now that this part is out of the way, are you ready for more fun?

What woman doesn't feel fabulous when she walks out of a hair salon with a fresh cut and blow dry? Or after putting on a hot red shade of lipstick? Or after swiping on some mascara that makes her eyes pop? It's time to learn how to polish up your look by using the right makeup with the right techniques, and finding hairstyles that suit you. If you haven't changed your hairstyle in twenty years or are still using bright blue eye shadow, girlfriend, it's time for a change!

> *I always hated swimsuit season because I am a tall, thigh heavy, flat-chested girl, and I've always had so much trouble finding a swimsuit. That is, until I recently found a swim skirt that fits longer on my thighs, as you recommended. I feel so good in it, and guess what? I'm not afraid of wearing a swimsuit anymore!*
>
> *Dawn*

Survival of the Smartest:

Make a Statement:
With Hair and Makeup

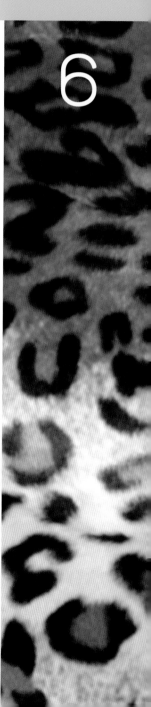

6

THE MOMENT OF TRUTH HAS ARRIVED. I WANT YOU TO BE completely honest with yourself and answer this question:

When was the last time you received a compliment on your hair?

Do you remember? If you can honestly say you can't remember, it's time to do something about it. As I once heard someone say, "It's time to cut it, dye it, or buy some more." I have a general rule I advise following. If you haven't received a compliment from a total stranger in the last two weeks (we're talking about a compliment from someone other than a family member), then it's time to start dialing that phone.

Your hair is one of, if not *the* first thing that someone notices about you. It's kind of like your calling card. Yours might be straight, curly, black, red, blonde, permed, braided, long, or short. Yours might be cut into the latest style or hanging in a ponytail down your back. Yours might be partially graying or almost completely gray. Whatever color, texture, or style your hair might have, it can look good. And it should.

Is Your Hairstyle Really Your Own?

Here's the thing I don't understand. Why do so many women (caution: this might be you) let their family members or others decide for her how she should wear her hair? Seriously, I don't get it. You wouldn't believe the number of women who tell me they *have* to be blonde (and their hair is really dark brunette) because their husband likes blonde hair. Or a woman tells me she isn't going to cut her hair because someone in her family likes it long. Or even better, a woman decides to keep dyeing her hair lighter because she read somewhere that women look better with lighter hair as they grow older.

Recently, a woman in her late forties asked me if I thought she should cut her long hair.

After assessing her face shape, hair texture, and age, I told her she certainly would look better with shorter hair, preferably in a length near her shoulders with more angles and layers. What she said next shouldn't have surprised me (because I hear it all the time), but it still did. This woman told me the reason she hadn't cut her hair is because her ten-year-old daughter liked it long. Yes, that's right, I said ten years old. I imagine this child was probably not a style expert by any means. But, wait, the story gets even crazier. Wouldn't you know it, the woman who asked me the question is in the fashion industry. And there she was, listening to her tween daughter telling her how she should wear her hair. Absolutely ridiculous.

Now I'm not saying you shouldn't have long hair if you're over a certain age. Some women can carry a longer style and look great. This is not the point. I want to know *why* you are wearing your hair the way you do. I hope you have chosen your cut and color because it is best suited for you and you love it. Not because your hubby, your coworker, your mother, or your adolescent daughter likes it that way.

> *Girl, you know you totally bossed me into getting my hair cut short again — and I completely love it! Everyone looks at my old pictures and comments how they like to see my face now. You rock!*
>
> *Amy*

Make a Statement:

Your Hairdresser Can Be Your New Best Friend

When I moved to North Carolina, I knew I had to immediately find a hair stylist, one that would take time with me and get to know my style, my hair texture, even my face shape. Moving is hard enough, but another challenge is finding a new stylist. I'm sure you know exactly what I'm talking about. Many of us have stylists that have become a part of our family. When we have to move to another part of the country and leave them, it can feel like losing a best friend.

So there I was in a new state thinking, "Who's going to do my hair like Michael?" (Michael was my hairstylist and wonder-worker when I lived in Miami.) Fortunately, after searching high and low, I finally found a stylist whom I could completely trust. I could sit down in her chair and be confident that I was going to leave the salon looking better than I did coming in. The story in how I ended up with her, though, is quite interesting. I'll get to that in a little bit.

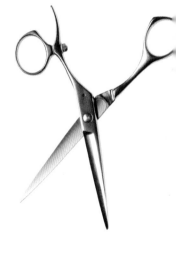

My hair has always been a sore spot for me. I can dress well and apply makeup like a pro, but when it comes to my hair, I will admit I'm pretty bad at it. I grew up with a very fashionable mother, one who not only knew how to dress and accessorize, but one that got her hair done every Friday. Yup, every Friday. There could be a major snowstorm on its way, but my mother would find a way to get to that hairdresser. She not only knew what looked good on her, but she knew what looked good on me and was never shy in letting me know. Yes, there are some family members whose style advice you can benefit from, but remember they are probably over ten years old and tend to be more stylish than the average woman.

My mother always knew when it was time for me to get my hair cut into a new style. When I was in high school, this really wasn't an issue because "high school hair" is just that … high school hair. You tend to wear it like everyone else and be done with it. This is not the case when you graduate from college and enter the adult world.

When I was in school and spent vacation breaks back home with my family, my mother would be the first person to tell me when my hair wasn't right. She'd say something subtle like, "Shari, you've GOT to do something with your hair!" It was how I knew it was time for an appointment. Before you start thinking my mom was a style piranha who ate less-fashionable folk alive, I want you to understand she was also the most complimentary person I've known. So I could definitely trust her advice. She was always right, anyway.

When I found Michael, my mother never said a bad word about my hair again. Instead she'd say, "Shari, you must NEVER leave this guy. I don't care if you have to fly back and forth to Miami to see him, you must never leave him." When I moved, of course, flying back and forth for hair appointments was ludicrous. I did get to visit Miami now and then, and I was able to sneak in appointments so he could "fix" the poor cuts and color jobs I got from the various hairdressers I tried out in my new home state.

I did this until the day I saw *her*. You might know who I'm talking about. It's the woman with the beautiful haircut and color you see walking down the street. Her locks are stunning, and before you know it, you start walking fast to catch up with her and admire her coiffure up close. As you close in, you wonder what you're going to say because you don't want to sound like a stalker. But you're desperate. You touch the mop of uneven frizz on your head and cast another glance at her luscious hair. You just have to ask. As you reach the stylish woman, you blurt out, "I LOVE your hair! Who does it and may I pleasssssssssssss-seeeeeeeeeeeeeee have her or his number?"

If you've never done something like that before, you might want to try it. Girls, it's really easy. I did and that's how I found my current stylist in North Carolina, Cindy Russell. The woman who sported the wonderful cut and color on the street? Her name was Tammy, and she changed my life. Okay, maybe I'm being a little dramatic.

If you haven't had a compliment in a while, look around your workplace, the mall, the coffee shop, the PTA meeting, the streets, wherever, and find someone who has a haircut that you admire and looks like she may have the same base color and texture as yours. Ask her who her stylist is and make an appointment. You'll be surprised how this will change the course of your hair.

Make a Statement:

Your Face, Your Shape

Most experts agree that there are four basic face shapes — oval, square, round, and heart. Keep in mind that figuring out what shape your face is can be subjective; this is not an exact science. You might think your face is one particular shape, while your best friend or sister sees another. If you have a good stylist, one who really understands not only hair, but also your face, head, and body shape, then she or he can design a fabulous style for you no matter what the shape of your face.

Oval

I've included pictures in this chapter so you can see the four face shapes in before and after shots. Even though we are showing only one style per face shape, this will give you a good starting point to give your stylist. She or he can take it from there.

Ready to find out what face shape you've got? Go get a notepad, something to write with, and your trusty tape measure. Also, you are going to want to do this exercise in front of a mirror on a wall, not a handheld one.

Square

STEP 1: Measure your face across the top of your cheekbones. Do this by placing one end of the tape measure just past the outside corner of your eye. Lay the tape across the bridge of your nose past the outside corner of your other eye. Make sure the tape measure is resting on the apples of your cheeks, on top of the cheekbones. Write down this number.

Round

STEP 2: Measure across your forehead at the widest point. Do this by placing the measuring tape about halfway between your eyebrows and your hairline. Write down this number.

STEP 3: Measure your jaw line next. Measure from your widest point to the widest point. Find the base just near your ear as your starting and ending point. Write down this number. Make sure you don't go all the way to your ears, you want to measure just to the ends of your face as you are looking straight on in the mirror.

Heart

STEP 4: Finally, measure the length of your face from your hairline to the bottom of your chin. Write down this number.

Now you can determine which face shape you have. You are:

Oval: if your face is approximately one and a half times as long as it is wide. (Measurements 3 and 4)

Square: if your forehead, cheekbones, and jaw line are almost equal in width. (Measurements 1, 2 and 3)

Round: if your face is almost as wide as it is long. The measurement does not have to be exact, but very close, usually within ¼" to ½". (Measurements 2 and 3 vs. 4)

Heart: if your face is wider at the forehead and cheekbones, but narrow at your jaw line. (Measurements 1 and 2 vs. 3)

Now it's time to people watch. Look around for women who seem to have the same face shape as you. Do you like their haircuts? I'd also recommend buying a magazine that features different hairstyles for face shapes. Cut out some pictures, take them to your stylist, and see what she or he thinks. Your stylist may think your face shape is different than what you think it is, and that's okay. The key is to decide together on a new look for you and try something based on what works for your face, your hair texture, and your age.

I have gone as far as to stop a woman in the mall because I loved her hairstyle. I even asked her if I could take her picture. Yes, I did! I was with my sister-in-law (and our girls who thought I was CRAZY). I told this woman I loved her cut and wanted to show it to my stylist. She was flattered!

Alyce

Make a Statement:

Here are a few points to remember based on your specific face shape:

Oval

You're certainly blessed if you have an oval face shape because most styles work for you. Make sure you are wearing a style that is age-appropriate and one that works with the texture of your hair.

An oval-shaped face with a "before" haircut

A great cut for an oval-shaped face!

A "before" haircut
for a square-shaped face

Avoid square-like hairstyles that will only make your face look harsh, such as cuts that end straight at your chin, or long, straight hair with no wave. You'll want cuts that have movement around the face, drawing attention to your cheekbones and creating softness at the jaw line. Fullness and lift at the crown will create balance. Short and medium-length haircuts are great for you.

A more flattering haircut for a square-shaped face

Make a Statement:

Round

Straight styles work very nicely, especially when height is added to your crown to create balance. Stay away from severe, short haircuts, as these will not flatter your round face. No center parts. Off-center parts with lots of layers look great on you. You'll also want to avoid fullness at your sides. Angled cuts work wonders on you. Try fringy cuts that are styled away from your face. You don't want anything styled flat and straight. Ponytails are a no-no.

A "before" haircut
for a round-shaped face

A great cut for a round face

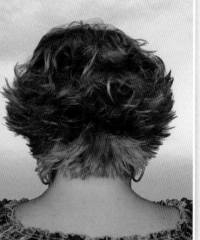

A "before" haircut
for a heart-shaped face

Bobs look awesome on you. Make sure your bob ends right at your chin, as this will create beautiful balance. Don't wear styles that have a lot of height at the crown, as this will make you look out of balance. Longer, below-the-shoulder length cuts are good too. Shaggier, fringy styles are super.

A more flattering style for a heart-shaped face

Make a Statement:

Choosing the Right Color

You are most beautiful when you are closest to the way God created you to be. That means if you are a natural redhead but you think you look better as a brunette, well, you are probably wrong.

In my travels, I mostly see women who dye their hair blonde who have no business being blonde at all. I suppose they all think blondes have more fun. Or perhaps it's the persuasions of society or their husband, mother, best friend, or boss who have convinced them that blonde is the way to go. Whatever the reason, you have to remember that not everyone is meant to be a blonde.

In chapter 2, where we covered the subject of color, I asked you what your natural hair color is. I'm sure many of you couldn't remember. If you insist on coloring your hair, then make sure you color it no more than two to three shades removed from that natural color. But there's more. Based on your dominant color characteristics, there are some simple rules that go hand-in-hand with each category regarding hair color.

LIGHT. Because you are a natural blonde, stay blonde. If your hair has turned white, I say, go with it! You are welcome to add more natural highlights to your hair, but always stay light. Darker hair won't cut it for you. As you turn gray, add subtle highlights to disguise the incoming strands.

DEEP. You are a natural brunette, most likely in the medium to dark range. Your hair may also be black. If you have lighter or gray hair and still fall into the Deep color category, it is because of the depth of your eyes. You have a tendency to want to add highlights, but I'd like to warn you against them. It's not that they're unattractive,

but it seems that most women in the Deep category seem to go overboard with their highlights. Feel free to add some high and lowlights to your hair, but always keep the frame around your face high- and lowlight-free. The depth of your coloring is what brings your eyes out.

WARM. Always keep red, copper, or warm golden coloring in your hair. As you mature, red hair seems to fade, so add stunning highlights to your hair. And always make sure it has a warm undertone. No ash for you. Ever.

COOL. Your silver, white, gray, or salt-and-pepper hair looks fabulous just as it is. My advice: leave it alone. If you choose to color it or add highlights, stay away from golden undertones.

CLEAR. You are the only one of all these categories who should never put highlights in your hair. Keep your hair color as dark as possible, as close to your natural shade, and watch your eyes pop. Trust me on this. If you insist on color, just add a high gloss for shine.

SOFT. With your soft, medium hair coloring, a few highlights and lowlights look very nice on you. Don't go too blonde or too dark. Stay very close to a medium intensity.

A stranger at church complimented my hair last Sunday. I have a short wedge cut and tend to get many compliments and people asking who cuts my hair. There are times when I want to grow it out long, but I know that I look better with shorter hair. The compliments help keep it how it should be! When I see a woman with a cute style, I definitely compliment her. It's the nice thing to do!

Kristin

Make a Statement:

Final Thoughts about Your Locks

You don't have to have short hair if you are over forty. Hair length should be based on your face shape, body shape, lifestyle, and age. Because the beauty industry is so advanced and women are using products more regularly than they did fifty years ago, we are about ten years ahead of what used to be considered old. Today's forty is the new thirty. Just make sure your hairstyle works for you and not against you.

A larger woman does not need itty-bitty hair (or extremely short hair). Strive for balance with your body and face and add some fullness.

Short hair will make a shorter woman appear taller. Most women should stay away from very long hair. Taller women, however, can have longer hair and still look balanced.

If you've got incoming gray hair and want to cover it up, try a semi-permanent color to get a glimpse of what you will look like with color. Semi-permanent color lasts about six weeks before the color fades. If you want to try something between washes, use a shampoo-in type color that will cover the gray AND wash out with your next shampoo. If you're totally in love with what the semi-permanent color did for you, then go with a permanent color to get back to your true color.

Your color will always stay longer and more vibrant when you use professional products (shampoo, conditioner, styling products) bought in your hair salon. The good news about these products is that they are so concentrated, a little goes a long way. Trust me, they are well worth the money.

If you want to add some brightness to your hair, no matter what color it is, try a color mousse or color-enhancing shampoo. This will make your blonde hair appear blonder, your red hair appear more red, and your brunette hair appear deeper and richer. These shampoos deposit small amounts of color on your hair to enhance your natural coloring, but shampoo out with each wash. You can buy them at retail stores like Target, Walmart, or most drug stores.

If you have to choose between getting your hair cut or getting your hair colored by a professional, you should opt for the haircut and then do your own color at home. When you think about it, you can have the most amazing color, but if your haircut stinks, then no matter what you do, it won't look good. A good haircut trumps good hair color every time. If you can afford to get both done by a professional, then by all means, go for it. If you can't afford both, perhaps you know someone with whom you can trade services. She can cut and color your hair, and you can clean her house every six weeks. I'm sure you have a gift or talent a hairstylist would love to have.

The average haircut should last four to six weeks. However, keep in mind that some shorter cuts need attention more often than that. So even though this might be the average, you know when you start feeling shaggy. If you want to keep the style you have, make sure you have it cut every four to six weeks. If you're trying to grow it out, then just get a trim every six to eight weeks.

Curly hair? Wish I had some. Embrace your curls and don't feel the need to straighten your hair all the time. Get a product like *Deva Curl* to help your curls stay soft and frizz-free. A good haircut is key for curly-haired gals. The tightness of your curls will determine what length layers you should have. To enjoy naturally curly hair, keep medium to long layers in your hair. Short layers will keep your curls tighter and curlier. Make sure your stylist never uses a razor on your curls, as this will split the ends and only cause it to frizz more. Shears are the only cutting tool that should touch your hair. A blunt cut will flatter you best and will allow you to wear it curly or blown out.

Curly or straight options

Make a Statement:

If you've been seeing the same stylist for years and you look the same today as you did five years ago, you need a change. You might first ask your regular stylist for her advice. She may have wanted to try something new on you for years, yet was afraid to mention the idea, thinking you might not like it. Give her (or him) a chance. Tell her to give you a cut and color she would recommend. If she has no ideas or keeps putting your request back into your hands, find someone new. Also, do as I suggested before and find a woman with a great look. Then make an appointment with her stylist and get an upgrade on your locks.

Recently, I got a fantastic letter from one of my blog readers, Cindy, from St. Petersburg.

Here is what she said:

Dear Shari,

I finally decided I needed a hair change. After taking several pictures with me to my stylist and discussing them with her, she gave me the cut and color I desperately needed. I have had so many compliments. A lot of my friends are also telling me I look younger — yippee! I should have done this forever ago. But better late than never, right? Now take a look at me. Colors that flatter me? Accessories? Great haircut and color? Feeling good about myself? Priceless! Thanks so much.

Cindy W.

Wow! That made me feel priceless!

So what about you? Are you ready to get an update on your haircut or get back to a natural color for your hair? Are you ready to look and feel priceless?

If you've been seeing the same stylist for years and you look the same today as you did five years ago, you need a change.

The Eyes Have It

In chapter 3, where I talked about accessories, I gave you some advice on how to choose sunglasses and referred to this chapter. Since we figured out what shape your face is, let me bring up the topic of eyewear. Choosing the right frames for your face is as important as having the right haircut or wearing the right color lip gloss. Here are some tips for choosing the right frame for your face shape.

Oval. The most important aspect in choosing eye frames is to make sure the proportions are correct. If you have smaller features, then make sure you choose a frame that has smaller lines. The opposite is also true. Try geometric, rectangle, cat eye, and butterfly styles. Find a color that complements your dominant color characteristic. The goal is to keep the balance of your oval face.

Square. Look for frames that will soften your angles and that are wider than the fullest part of your face. Recommended shapes for you include round, cat eyes, semi-rimless, and narrow ovals — all these shapes will soften your face. Remember to purchase a pair that complements your beautiful natural coloring.

Glasses options for an oval-shaped face

Frames that work for a square-shaped face

Make a Statement:

Great styles
for a round face

Round. Because of your round face, you'll want to choose glasses that have a more angular look to them. Look for frames that are octagonal, rectangular, or square. Mid to high temples will lengthen your face. Look for glasses that have some color to them, always remembering to buy a pair that is complementary to your dominant color characteristic. Rectangular and geometric-shaped frames will make your face appear slimmer.

Heart. The most important feature on your frames is that they must be wider at the bottom than they are at the top; this will balance your heart-shaped face. Cat-eye styles are super on you, as well as butterfly and round styles. Look for frames that have lower temples for additional balance. Avoid frames that are decorative on top. Always remember to buy a pair that is complementary to your natural coloring.

Flattering glasses for
a heart-shaped face

Making Up Is Not Hard to Do

Makeup. It can be a woman's nightmare or her saving grace. It can be intimidating or a welcome breath of fresh air. It can be a chance to look like a clown or beautifully flatter her best features. What about you? Is makeup your friend or foe?

However you feel about this subject, I'm here to tell you that no face is complete without a little makeup. You may think it's okay to run out of your house bare-faced while doing routine errands like grocery shopping or taking your kids to soccer practice. Nope. Trust me, even a little makeup goes a long way. Applying a swipe of gloss and a coat of mascara will do wonders for your looks, believe you me. Get used to this truth, friend: makeup makes everyone look better. Period.

During the daytime, you can wear minimal makeup while you're at home or running errands. Aim for a little powder for coverage, lip gloss, and mascara. Feel free to wear more if you like.

Nighttime is when you can really glam it up. Wear foundation and powder, darker eyeliner, lipstick, and gloss. You can also get creative and wear bolder colors. Be sure that you only do that with one area of your face, leaving the rest a little more natural. For example, if you are going with a dark eye or smoky look, just swipe on some gloss. If you want to wear a bright lip gloss, just wear a natural shade of eye shadow and some mascara. However you decide to play up your face, don't be afraid to wear a little more makeup at night, because the lighting is dimmer and you need a little more to show up on your face.

Now that we've got that settled, here is what every makeup wardrobe should include:

Concealer. This product is worn to conceal blemishes, skin imperfections, and dark under-eye circles. Choose a color one shade lighter than your skin tone and foundation color.

Makeup Primer. Though this is an optional product and you don't have to use it, it helps to make sure your makeup will glide on and stay on. This is a product that you apply after you've applied your moisturizer and before you put on your foundation. My favorites are Lancôme's

> *I accentuate my natural features so much better now that I know about my colors for makeup and clothing!*
>
> *Christy*

La Base Pro Perfecting Makeup Primer and Smashbox's Photo Finish Foundation Primer, but you also might like Pixi's Brightening Primer, which you can find at Target.

Foundation, Powder, or Both. Foundation is worn to help your skin appear more flawless. I think it's a must for most women over thirty. Foundation color should be as close to the natural shade of your skin as possible. Test foundation on your jaw line or neck. Mineral powder is a wonderful product that can be used in place of foundation. This powder can also be used over foundation to set your makeup. You may also choose pressed powder to carry in your purse so you can touch up your makeup throughout the day, or opt for the loose powder for one-time application.

Blush. Blush is worn to give color to your cheeks. It comes in powder or creamy consistencies in shades complementary to your natural coloring. Apply with a brush or fingertips.

Lip Liner. This is a pencil specifically designed to use around the outside edges of your lips before applying your lipstick or gloss.

Lipstick, Lip Gloss, or Both. Lipstick comes in light to heavy coverage formulas in natural tones with a cool or warm undertone and should be chosen based on your dominant color characteristic. Clear lip gloss can enhance your lipstick shade, or tinted gloss can be worn alone or used to change the color of your lipstick.

Eyebrow Pencil or Brow Powder. Filling in your eyebrows with color is a must for most women. It is one of the best anti-aging tricks you can do. You can use a pencil or a brow powder for this.

Eyeliner. This product can be worn along your bottom lash line, your top lash line, or both to frame your eyes.

Eyeshadow. Wear eyeshadow to enhance your own eyes, not to distract. Don't wear shades the exact same color as your eyes. You can choose to wear one shade, usually in a lighter skin tone color for a finished look, or wear two to four colors at a time.

Mascara. A must for most women. Mascara lengthens and adds volume to eyelashes. A great accessory is an eyelash curler. Curl your lashes before applying mascara and your eyes will pop.

Your Best Colors Now

Here are the colors you should wear based on your dominant color characteristics:

LIGHT

Concealer: Light ivory or ivory

Foundation, powder, or both: Color should be the same as your skin tone

Blush: A light natural pink or peachy tone

Lipstick, lip gloss, or both, and lip liner: Soft shades of pinks, peaches, plums, or natural browns

Eyeliner: Medium brown, charcoal gray, plum

Eyeshadow: For blue eyes, try shades of brown, peach, and natural taupe; for green or hazel eyes, try browns, beiges, and light shades of plum or violet; for brown, black, or gray eyes, try rose tones, peaches, shades of gray, and soft browns.

Eyebrow color: Blonde pencil or brow powder

Mascara: Brown or black, your preference

DEEP

Concealer: Light to medium beige

Foundation, powder, or both: Color should be the same as your skin

Blush: Medium shades of plum or natural hues of brown or brick

Lipstick, lip gloss, or both, and lip liner: Neutrals, berries, plum

Eyeliner: Dark brown or black

Eyeshadow: For blue eyes, try shades of brown, peach, and natural taupe; for green or hazel eyes, try browns, beiges, and deep shades of plum or violet; for brown, black, or gray eyes, try rose tones, peaches, shades of gray, golds, and rich browns.

Eyebrow color: Brown brow pencil or brow powder

Mascara: Brown or black, your preference

WARM

Concealer: Ivory, beige, or bronze

Foundation, powder, or both: Color should be same as your skin tone

Blush: Coral, brown, peach, brick

Lipstick, lip gloss, or both, and lip liner: Copper, neutral, brown, peach

Eyeliner: Brown, bronze, green

Eyeshadow: For blue eyes, try shades of brown, peach, and natural taupe; for green or hazel eyes, try browns, beiges, and medium shades of plum or violet; for brown, black, or gray eyes, try peaches, shades of gray, golds, and warm browns. Add a touch of copper or gold to your eyelids for beautiful shine.

Eyebrow color: Blonde or soft auburn pencil or brow powder

Mascara: Brown or black, your preference

COOL

Concealer: Ivory or beige

Foundation, powder, or both: Color should be same as your skin tone

Blush: Pink, plum, rose, berry

Lipstick, lip gloss or both, and lip liner: Shades of pink, plum, berry

Eyeliner: Black, charcoal, navy, plum

Eyeshadow: For blue eyes, try shades of pinks, ivory, and natural taupes; for green or hazel eyes, try rose or silver gray and medium shades of plum or violet; for brown, black, or gray eyes, try rose tones or soft black.

Eyebrow color: Soft black or brown pencil or brow powder; color should be same as your eyebrows

Mascara: Black or navy

I have never really worn a lot of makeup. But learning about my colors and how to wear makeup made a huge difference in how I feel about myself. Now I want to eat better and exercise and wear nice clothes. It just makes me feel better about myself.

April

Concealer: Ivory, beige, or deep beige

Foundation, powder, or both: Color should be same as your skin tone

Blush: Neutral, soft rose, plum

Lipstick, lip gloss or both, and lip liner: Berries, neutrals, high-shine glosses

Eyeliner: Black, navy, plum, dark brown

Eyeshadow: For blue eyes, try shades of brown, peaches, and roses; for green or hazel eyes, try browns, beiges, and medium shades of plum or violet; for brown, black, or gray eyes, try rose tones, peaches, shades of gray, silver, or crystalline colors.

Eyebrow color: Soft black or brown pencil or brow powder

Mascara: Black

SOFT

Concealer: Ivory or medium beige

Foundation, powder, or both: Color should be the same as your skin tone

Blush: Medium shades of peach or rose

Lipstick, lip gloss, or both, and lip liner: Medium shades of neutrals, peaches, pinks, browns

Eyeliner: Brown, bronze, plum, charcoal

Eyeshadow: For blue eyes, try shades of brown, peach, and natural taupe; for green or hazel eyes, try browns, beiges, and medium shades of plum or violet; for brown, black, or gray eyes, try rose tones, peaches, shades of gray, golds, and medium browns.

Eyebrow color: Blonde or light brown brow pencil or brow powder

Mascara: Brown or black, your preference

Make a Statement:

Great Skin Starts Here

The most important component to a beautiful face is proper skincare. I am an absolute maniac when it comes to this. My most obsessive (and rightfully so) skincare regimen is that I never go to bed with my makeup on. And neither should you. I was once told that for every night you leave your makeup on, your skin ages seven days. Yikes! Whether that's true or not, it was enough to scare me to the sink every night to wash off that stuff.

There are so many brands of skincare, finding the right products for you may be an overwhelming experience. I know the feeling. My very first job in college was working in the cosmetics department of a large department store in Miami, Florida. I was called a "flyer," which meant I was the girl who had to work in whatever area I was needed. Basically I filled in for whoever didn't show up that day.

As I flew from counter to counter, I learned about every single cosmetic brand this department store carried. I worked with lines such as Clinique, Estée Lauder, Revlon, Chanel, and many others. Looking back, I see God's hand in that. I tried all different brands and never stuck to one particular product line.

After graduating, I got a full-time job with this same store working for Elizabeth Arden. Shortly after that time, I was offered a management job with a specialty store in South Miami, where I spent the next seven years. I was in charge of the entire department where we sold products by Lancôme, Borghese, Elizabeth Arden, and Clarins, as well as men's and women's fragrances. This turned me into a product junkie and made me very knowledgeable about cosmetics and skincare.

After moving to North Carolina, I got a job with Estée Lauder before deciding to try my hand at Mary Kay. I was pretty good at selling Mary Kay. I earned three pink Cadillacs in my first seven years with the company! You bet I did. I'm no longer an active part of the Mary Kay world because God had another plan for me to speak and write, but I have to confess something to you.

It was very hard for me to make the decision to sell Mary Kay because I was what you might call a "cosmetic snob." As a matter of fact, I didn't tell any of my friends I was selling Mary Kay because I was afraid they would laugh at me. See, when I worked at the fancy stores with the fancy products, I snubbed the women who used what I thought were inferior brands like Mary Kay or even Avon. I thought, "Who in the world would wear those brands?" I'm embarrassed to think I acted so haughty. Many of their products have since become favorites of mine!

I recently discovered Rodan+Fields anti-aging skincare and I'm loving the compliments I'm receiving on my younger-looking skin. I'm very impressed with these products, but there are many good skincare products out there. The important thing is to be sure and use one!

All that being said, let's find out what's important in a skincare regimen.

You must use products that are designed for your skin type. Do you have dry, oily, normal, or a combination of these skin types? Here's an easy way to tell what type you have:

STEP 1: Wash your face with a gentle soap or cleanser, rinse, and gently pat dry.

STEP 2: Wait about an hour. Don't apply any makeup during this time.

STEP 3: Note whether your skin feels tight.

STEP 4: Tissue time. Press a separate single-ply tissue onto each of the following areas of your face: center of forehead, outer forehead, chin, center of cheeks, outer cheeks, and nose.

STEP 5: Examine each tissue and check for any oily residue or flaky skin residue.

STEP 6: Determine your skin type.
- Oil on each tissue indicates you have oily skin.

- Oil on only some tissues (especially on the center of forehead, nose, chin, and center of cheeks) indicates you have combination skin.
- Flaky skin residue on all tissues, without any oily residue, means you have dry skin.
- Tight skin without any oily residue indicates a dry skin type.
- No oil, no flaky residue, and no tightness in your skin indicate you have a normal skin type.

Once you have determined your skin type, it's time to choose skincare products.

Sensitive. You have sensitive skin if you have skin that is easily irritated, delicate, thin, and prone to allergic reactions, or if your capillaries show through your skin. It is important you choose products specifically for sensitive skin. One brand I'd recommend for you to try is Clarins. Products like the Gentle Foaming Cleanser, Extra-Comfort Toning Lotion, and Gentle Day and Night Cream are extremely delicate on your sensitive skin. Another good one to try is Aveda's All-Sensitive Cleanser and Moisturizer.

Another sign of delicate skin is acne. (And you thought pimples were just for teenagers!) If you are suffering from acne, make sure to use products that are designed for sensitive skin and stay away from anything that is scented. Sometimes just good old-fashioned water is the only relief you'll get until your skin settles down. Try a product from the Cetaphil or Curel lines.

Normal or Slightly Oily to Dry. Believe it or not, about 75 percent of women are said to have a normal skin type. For those of you who fall into this category or who may have slightly oily skin ranging to slightly dry skin, yet still require anti-aging products, I recommend Redefine by Rodan+Fields or the Timewise Miracle Set by Mary Kay. Your skin will thank you for it. If you insist on shopping at the mall, Origins has an antioxidant line called A Perfect World that will get your skin looking fresh and renewed.

Oily or Acne. If you are one of those folks who has very oily skin and acne, you should try Avon's Clearskin Professional Acne Treatment System. It works wonders on skin prone to breakouts. There is an additional product that I think every person who ever gets a pimple (or lots of them) should have. It's Mary Kay's Acne Treatment Gel and it costs about ten bucks. As soon as you feel a blemish coming on, you spot treat it with this product several times a day and, voila, within 24 – 36 hours, the blemish is gone. My teenage son even uses it. Neutrogena's Oil Free Acne Wash Pink Grapefruit Foaming Scrub and Rapid Clear Acne Defense Face Lotion are highly recommended too.

As far as a beauty regimen you should follow, here is a basic suggestion of how to care for your skin on a regular basis.

Morning Routine

- Cleanser
- Toner (Some cleansers contain a built-in toner so you may get to skip this step)
- Daytime anti-aging treatment (optional)
- Moisturizer with sunscreen

Bedtime Routine

- Eye makeup remover
- Cleanser
  - Night time anti-aging treatment (optional)
    - PM moisturizer or night cream
      - Eye cream

Make a Statement:

- Microdermabrasion (this will exfoliate your skin)
- Exfoliators or masks if part of your skincare system (if you are using a microdermabrasion system, you won't need extra masks and exfoliators)

It's most important to stick with one product line. For example, don't use a different brand of cleanser, toner, and moisturizer as part of your regimen. Skincare systems are just that — systems. They are meant to be used together and will be most effective when you do.

This is not true for makeup. With cosmetics, feel free to experiment with any brand you'd like. I found, however, that it's always easier to stick with one brand across the board. It makes beauty time simple.

Girlfriend, please take care of your skin. It's crucial. You only have one face, and if it goes completely dry and wrinkly on you because you've used and abused it, there's not much you can do about it. Also, always wear sunscreen and don't bake in the sun. If you have some bad habits like excessive smoking and drinking, remember these wreak havoc on your skin, so my advice is to give them up. I know, I know — it's easier said than done.

Finally, don't give up on a skincare system a week after you've started using it. You need to give it time, at least four weeks, to work. Your skin may break out slightly or start flaking, but that's okay; it means the product is working. It's cleaning it out and pushing things to the surface. If your skin starts to burn and itch, stop using the product immediately.

It's most important to stick with one skincare product line.

Can't Stop the Age . . .
Can Do a Little Somethin'
About the Process

Listen. We're all getting older. There's no way to stop time. There's no way to completely eliminate wrinkles. There's no way to make laugh lines disappear. And while there is no anti-aging product out there that will miraculously give you back the skin you had when you were in high school, there are some tricks you can use to help you look a little younger than you are. Take my advice and see for yourself the difference these suggestions can make.

Eyebrows. If you are one of those girls who doesn't do a thing with your eyebrows because you don't see the need, you might want to think again. Proper eyebrow grooming is one of the quickest ways to make you look younger and more polished. You might need to tweeze a few gray hairs out of your brows or you may need to wax them to get them into a good shape. Whatever you decide to do, remember that eyebrows frame your eyes and your face, and grooming them properly and regularly will do wonders for your looks. After the age of thirty, most women need to fill in their eyebrows with either a brow pencil (most cosmetic lines carry them) or brow powder so their brows don't look sparse. If you've never done this before, try filling in one eyebrow with a color very close to that of your brows and cover up the other eye to peer in a mirror. See what it looks like when one eyebrow is filled in and the other isn't. It's amazing, isn't it? I'd recommend going to a professional to get your eyebrows shaped. It is well worth it and you'll look so good.

Facial hair. We all have some and if you don't yet, just wait. Even the least hairy of us get some pesky whiskers on our chins and upper lip area. Don't get grossed out. It's normal. It's what happens as we age. I recommend tweezing the chin hairs if you only have a few, but consider getting them waxed off by a professional if you have more than a couple. Also, when a professional (found at most hair and nail salons)

Make a Statement:

does this for you, the results last much longer. And, WOW, you'll look absolutely fabulous.

Foundation. As we age, we might feel we need to wear more foundation to cover up our wrinkles, but the opposite is true. I don't think you ever need heavy foundation, no matter your age, unless you have some serious skin imperfections like deep acne scars or burns that can only get covered up with this type of makeup. To look smooth skinned, consider wearing a light to medium coverage foundation and finish with a loose powder. Some mineral powders work well as a foundation, so try one and see if you like it. Some to try: Estée Lauder, M·A·C, and Bare Minerals.

Sunscreen. A must! No ifs, ands, or buts about it. Make sure you apply sunscreen with at least an SPF 15 when you are going to spend any time outdoors. I'd even recommend buying your moisturizer or anti-aging serum with an SPF 15 or higher so you wear it automatically each day. Some to try: Clinique, Estée Lauder, Rodan+Fields, and Aveeno.

Microdermabrasion. This treatment can be done by a licensed professional in a salon or you can purchase an at-home kit. Microdermabrasion helps reduce the appearance of fine lines, helps your pores to appear smaller, reduces the appearance of skin imperfections, and helps your skin to look beautifully smooth. This anti-aging treatment should be used approximately one to two times per week. A few to try: Mary Kay (my ultimate favorite), Olay Regenerist, and Lancôme.

Eye Cream. A must-have for any skincare regimen. Because the skin around your eyes is so delicate, it is important to use a cream specifically designed for this area. If you've ever noticed little white bumps near your eye area, this happens because you've used your regular moisturizer or night cream on this delicate skin, and because there are no oil glands in this area, you get an oil build up. Yikes! Make sure whatever eye cream you are using says just that, "eye" cream. Some of my faves include: Clarins, Elizabeth Arden, and Avon's Anew.

Neck. Treat your neck as you would your face. Keep it moisturized!

I'll bet some of you are reading this at nighttime, so before you forget (and unless you want your skin to age seven days tonight), go and wash off all that makeup and moisturize.

What is the one staple that most of us have a hundred pair of but none fit right? That's right, jeans. Jeans are one of those items that we all long to have the perfect pair of, but they seem to elude us. Skinny jeans, low-riders, bootcut, dark rinse, light rinse, five pocket, no pockets, flare, wide-leg. So many different styles, what to choose?

No worries. I'm here to help you find the perfect pair of jeans ... on the next page.

Make a Statement:

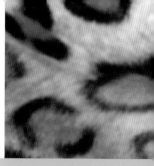

Jeans:
A Girl's Real Best Friend

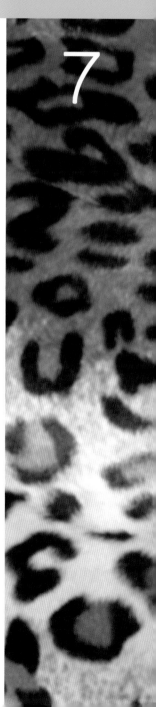

7

LET'S TAKE A TRIP TO YOUR CLOSET. I WANT TO LOOK INSIDE and see what you've got. Really, though, I want to see all your jeans. Count how many pairs you have and I'll bet you come up with at least three. You got more? If so, you are like most women across America and beyond. We love our jeans, don't we? Though most of us own quite a few pair, doesn't it seem that none of them fit just right? Ugh. It's so frustrating!

As I sat here today to write this chapter, I prayed for you. See, God has entrusted me with providing you valuable information and I want to make sure I do it the right way. I take this style business very seriously and, like I did for this entire book, I asked God to show me what to write that will help you. Because I'm sure you are like the many other women who ask me this question at almost all of my conferences and retreats: "How do I find a great-fitting pair of jeans?"

I know firsthand how hard it is to find the right ones. For starters, I'm 5'11", so mine need to be long. I'm also a b body type so I've got to cover my tummy. With low-rise jeans so prominent in the department stores, it's hard to find the rise that fits my body best. Trust me, the low-rise jeans don't cut it. Also, I don't have much in my trunk, so it's important my backside doesn't look as flat as a pancake. So rest assured, I probably have as much trouble as you finding a pair of jeans that serves all my needs.

I want you to be able to read this chapter and know just what to do when you are at your wit's end trying to find the perfect pair. I did a lot, I mean a LOT of research on jeans. I talked to experts and read as many style books as I could find on the topic, and they all left me feeling a little, well, overwhelmed. I certainly don't want to do that to you.

For example, I'm not sure you need to know, or even care to know, all the terms associated with this article of clothing. Does it really matter to you what "left hand twill" or "yarn-dyed cloth" means? I didn't think so. All you need to know is what will look good on you. That's it!

For starters, it's important to understand that one pair of jeans will not cover all your needs. Since jeans are acceptable for so many different occasions and can easily be dressed down or up, your basic wardrobe should include at least three pairs of good-fitting jeans, not three or more pairs of so-so fitting jeans. Here are the three types you should have in your closet:

- One pair in a dark wash to wear with heels
- One pair in a medium to dark wash to wear with flats
- One pair in a medium wash to wear with casual shoes or tennis shoes

Next you have to understand the different cuts of jeans so you know what they mean when you start shopping for your favorite pair.

Skinny

Straight

Bootcut

Jeans:

The cut of your jeans refers to how they are shaped: specifically, the style of the legs. Here are some terms you should be familiar with before you run out to the stores:

Narrow/Skinny Jean. Slim thigh, tapered at ankle. This jean is tight throughout the body of the jean, from the top all the way to the ankle.

Straight. Same width at thigh, knee, and leg opening. These jeans have a uniform fit from the top of the pant leg, at your thigh, to the very bottom of your leg. The bottom does not flare out, nor does it come in at the ankle.

Bootcut. Slightly flared to fit over boots. Bootcut jeans are slim in the thigh area and begin to angle out just below the knee and then moderately flare out at the bottom hem.

Flare. Narrow at knee with flared opening. Like bootcut jeans, flare-leg jeans angle out below the knee, but much more so, creating a bell-like shape at the hem. They are sometimes called wide leg.

Boyfriend. Loose, comfortable, straight, boxy. This cut refers to the style that looks like you borrowed your man's jeans. It has a straight shape that's thin through the hip, yet comfortably sits below the waist.

It's important to understand that one pair of jeans will not cover all your needs.

Flare

Boyfriend

Your Jeans Shopping Experience

Pick a day to head to the mall or a particular store to buy some jeans. You'll want to follow the shopping guide for jeans, included in this chapter on pages 156 – 59, which will guide you to the brands you should look for based on your body type. I've done extensive research on jeans shopping based on flattering the different figures, so trust me when I tell you which brands and stores will work for you. Decide on your budget, but don't be afraid to try on jeans that are a bit more expensive than what you usually buy. Compare the fit and feel of the higher and lower-priced jeans and decide which is worth it. Just like shopping for swimsuits, leave your kids at home and take a good friend with you who can offer some objective style and fit advice.

Here are a few tips to prepare you for your shopping and trying-on adventure. Are you ready?

Concentrate on looking for only one pair at a time, as this will save you lots of frustration.

Don't be afraid to spend some time trying on many different pairs. You're probably not going to love the very first pair you try, so trying on a few will help you understand what you like and don't like about jeans.

Wear the underwear you typically wear with slacks so you can see how they fit under your jeans. Bring your shaper along so you can see what your jeans look like with and without it. Wear a simple blouse or sweater.

Decide ahead of time what purpose these jeans will have and bring the shoes you plan to wear with them. If you're not sure, bring a pair that has the heel height you think you'll wear with them.

Take a measuring tape with you. You're going to measure some zippers. The rise of jeans is measured by the length of the zipper. Different rises either enhance or take away from a woman's body shape. Here is what I mean:

Super low-rise jeans have a one- to two-inch zipper and the waistband sits four to five inches below the navel.

Low-rise jeans have a three- to four-inch zipper and the waistband sits two to three inches below the navel.

Mid-rise jeans have a five- to six-inch zipper and the waistband sits right at the navel or just below it.

High-rise jeans have a seven- to eight-inch zipper and the waistband sits above the natural waistline, covering your navel.

I love, love, love my new jeans! After understanding the size zipper to look for, I felt empowered with new knowledge. I even knew more than the sales clerks! I only had to try on a few pairs before I found the perfect ones.

Wendi

What Will Work for Your Body Type

Jeans for a **b** body type

The most important thing to understand when shopping for your body is to cover your fluff. Low-rise will not work for you. Find jeans that cover your midsection so your muffin top is not falling over the edges of the waistband. I'm sure you'll agree when I say it's not a pretty sight, nor is it comfortable. Look for jeans that have pockets or decorations on the backside. Those with flaps and buttons are even better as this will make your bottom appear less flat. Mid-rise is best for you. Try brands with a little bit of Lycra as this helps hold down some tummy movement —you know, the stuff that jiggles. Straight legs, relaxed fit, and bootcut styles are good types to look for.

Jeans for an **o** body type

As an **o** body type, look for jeans that will minimize your lower and upper midsection. Because of your fuller upper body, balance is key for you. Finding jeans that form a straight line is important in achieving that balance. No skinny or wide-leg jeans for you. Stay in between these two styles and stick with relaxed fit and bootcut. Mid-rise should be your rise of choice. Stay away from high-rise as the waist will hit too high on your **o** body shape. Jeans that have at least 4 percent Lycra will help flatten your midsection. Consider wearing a tummy shaper or camisole shaper when wearing most of your clothes; this will help you to achieve a slimmer line.

Jeans:

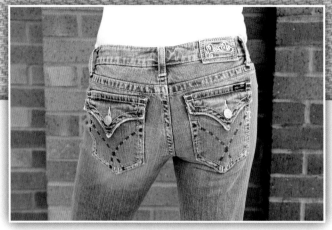

Flap pockets are great for **b** body types.

*Pockets for **b** and **o** body types,
or anyone with a flat bottom:*

- Flap pockets with buttons
- Pockets that are not too far apart
- Pockets with decorations in a vertical or curvy design
- Bottoms of pockets must hit right where your bottom starts to curve under.

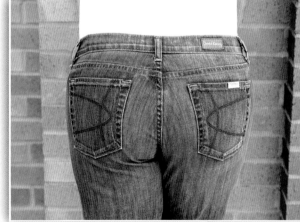

Pockets with vertical decoration are great for an **o** body type.

Jeans for a **d** body type

Your challenge is trying to find a pair of jeans that fit your hips, thighs, and waist. My suggestion is to find a pair that fits great on your hips and thighs, and then take the waist in, if necessary. If this sounds like too much trouble, have no fear. You'll be happy to know I've found some great styles for you that will fit these three parts of your body (included toward the end of this chapter in the shopping guide). I've done the work for you, so all you have to do now is go try them on and see if you like them.

Stay away from jeans that hug your hips and thighs, as this will bring attention to the area you are trying to minimize. Look for jeans that have a relaxed fit so they don't cling to your bottom half, but will instead balance this part of your body. Stay away from decorative pockets and pockets with flaps; these will make your rear look bigger. The plainer the pocket, the better. If your pocket does have a decoration, make sure it isn't a horizontal line or embellishment, but one that is more curvy or vertical in shape. Low-rise works wonders for you because you don't have to worry about it fitting at your waist. High-rise shows off your small waist. Jeans with a slight flare at the bottom will balance your body nicely. Remember, you'll always want to wear shoulder pads in your tops to create the illusion of an **x** body.

This plain-pocket jean is great for a **d** body type.

Pockets for **d** body types, or anyone with a big booty:

- Large pockets will make your booty look smaller
- No flaps or buttons
- Small designs on mid-size pockets
- Choose pockets that are proportionally sized and spaced on your bottom; simple designs on pockets are best.

Jeans for an **x** body type

You have a balanced body. So buy jeans that flatter you yet diminish any challenges you might have. Since you may gain a little extra in the tummy every now and then, keep in mind you might want to wear a shaper to camouflage this area. Flare legs look great on most body types, but then again, you can get away with wearing most any leg style, from skinny to wide leg. All rises work for you, so you might want to try on a few of each to see what works best. To make your life easier, stick with the choices I give you in the upcoming shopping guide.

Pockets for **x** body types

- Pockets should be proportionate to your shape and size.

- Mid-size designs on mid-size pockets work well.

- Keep in mind the line of the design on the pocket and where it leads your eye … in, out, up, or down. If your bottom tends to be a little wider, keep the design traveling inward, not outward. Vertical designs work nicely.

Great pockets for an **x** body type

- Bottoms of pockets should hit right where your bottom starts to curve under.

Fast Fixes for a Flattering Fit

Problem areas? I have your solutions right here!

Short waist: Elongate your look with a low waist. Flat front trouser-style jeans with side slash pockets are a perfect choice for you, though they are sometimes hard to find.

Long waist: Mid-rise to high-rise jeans with a straight leg balance your body.

Short legs: Low-rise with narrow legs are super on you. Wear with high heels or boots. Stay away from wide-leg jeans.

Long legs: Flare, bootcut, and narrow legs are your best choices. Opt for a mid-rise for balance. Break up your look with a top in a different color than your jeans.

Fluffy tummy: Follow the rules for the **b** body type.

Heavy thighs: Stick with a solid color wash, without any variations in the color.

*I am loving my new jeans! I am a combination **b** and **o** body type and I've always felt so frumpy and fat in jeans. I took your advice and bought a pair of Not Your Daughter's Jeans, and oh my goodness, I never knew I could look so good! I better go get another pair because I'm going to wear these out!*

Randi

Comfort is key! Sit down, jump around, and bend over. How do they feel?

No bubbling, please. (Bubbling is a term I invented to help girls and teens understand the fit of jeans. I teach it when I talk to girls about modesty.) Turn around and check out the backs of your thighs. Are your jeans so tight that you have lines of bubbling across the back? See the photo to see what I mean by bubbling.

Lift your shirt and check for a muffin top. If you have spillage, try a different rise or get a shaper to suck in the fluff.

Check the front of your jeans, just under your waistband and zipper area. Look in the mirror and see how it fits across the front and width. It should be a smooth fit, no stretched fabric and no loose fabric either.

The darker the denim, the thinner you look and the dressier the jeans appear.

Very few women look good in skinny jeans, unless you're very skinny or you're wearing them with a long top or jacket.

Your jeans should not be so tight you look poured into them. On the other hand, they shouldn't be too loose either.

An example of bubbling

Shopping Guide for Jeans

Try the brands below for your particular body type. You can find many of these in popular department stores or shops of the same brand. You can check online to find a local retailer. I've also listed a couple of places that sell particular brands.

b *body type*

1. *Old Navy "The Dreamer" Boot Cut Jeans* ($35) An inside tummy panel slims your tummy while flap back pockets add interest to your backside, all in a price that won't break the bank.

2. *Lee Slender Secret* ($20) No more muffin top! The built-in tummy control panels in these surprisingly stylish higher-rise jeans help eliminate stomach bulge, while hidden elastic in the waistband prevents gapping. And check out the incredibly low price!

3. *Rocha Slender Secret Barely Boot Jean* ($54) Don't waste your time fussing with your waistband; the Rocha Barely Boot jeans won't just accept your curves, they'll hug 'em, all the while saying bye bye to love handles.

4. *Not Your Daughter's Jeans* ($120 – $140) Always a winner for **b** body shapes as this firms and fits your body with a built-in system that minimizes your tummy and makes you look a size or two smaller. You will love these jeans.

5. *Paige Premium Denim Skyline* ($168) This mid-rise jean falls just below the belly button and stays put around the waist, thanks to a blend of cotton and luxury fiber (Dow XLA). The stretching power of XLA keeps this jean's shape longer — no unflattering bagging when you bend down or sit.

o *body type*

1. ***Dress Barn WESTPORT Collection*** ($30 – $40) A fit that never fails will make this pair your new favorite. Sits at the waist, slightly fitted through the hip and thigh. Check out Dress Barn's Roz&Ali dressier jeans too.

2. ***Catherine's Secret Slimmer Jean*** ($50 – $70) The classic Secret Slimmer jean has a straight leg style featuring a hidden tummy-control panel to slim your shape. Includes a smooth, contoured waistband and stretch denim fabric for ultimate comfort and fit.

3. ***Michael Kors "Sausalito" Bootcut Jean*** ($80) Get a designer jean at a fraction of the cost in these stylish denim darlings. You won't want just one pair. Honest.

4. ***Lane Bryant T3 collection*** ($70) T3's tummy-taming panel and hidden elastic waistband give each pair in this collection a flat out fabulous fit! They come in skinny, straight, and bootcut. A winner. Try Lane Bryant's Genius Fit collection too.

5. ***MiracleBody by MiracleSuit*** ($110) The 40% stretch fabric is wonderful for all over body slimming. Opt for black or dark denim for a dressier option. These follow your curves in the most wonderful way and will make you feel like a million bucks!

> *I am a* **b** *body type and believe it or not, Walmart has my favorite jeans! They are petite (for us short girlies), bootcut, AND stretch! And all for the lovely price of $15! Whoo hoo!*
>
> *Nicki*

d *body type*

1. *Riders by Lee* ($20) I'd be remiss not to include these terrific jeans for the gal with fuller hips and thighs. They instantly slim you with a no-gap waist, tummy control panel, and slimming stretch denim. Available at Walmart and Kmart.

2. *Levi's Jeans, 529 Curvy Bootcut Jeans* ($54) Perfect for the curvy girl, these jeans fit with little-to-no gap in the back. The slight flare to the bootcut leg will even out your figure and give you a balanced shape.

3. *Not Your Daughter's Bootleg Trouser Pant* ($108) Trouser-style jeans are cut wider through the upper leg, so they're a perfect choice to lengthen legs and hips. The extra stretch in this pick helps smooth and slim, particularly in the thigh and rear area.

4. *MiracleBody by MiracleSuit Samantha Jeans* ($110) The strategically placed embroidered pockets sit higher on the butt, drawing the eye up — and giving the area a visual lift. These jeans also contain 4 percent Lycra, which provides extra holding power in the rear … and all over.

5. *CJ by Cookie Johnson "Grace" Jeans* ($191) A pair that can handle your curves! This style's incredibly forgiving boot cut helps balance out full hips and thighs. And the near-magic cotton-and-elastin blend offers just the right amount of stretch, hugging skin without leaving any unsightly bumps.

x *body type*

1. *Levi's 518 Boot Cut Jeans* ($45 – $50) These fit true to size. The weight is not too light and has a bit of stretch. These are very flattering and promise to be your go-to jeans.

2. *Gap 1969 Denim* ($59 – 69) A premium fit, this jean is always comfortable and always fashionable. Whether you wear them with a silk blouse or graphic tee, this jean will take you anywhere you want to go in high style.

3. ***Ann Taylor Modern Boot Cut Jeans*** ($88) Five pocket styling combined with a sophisticated dark wash make these jeans a versatile basic. Wear this jean with flats for day or trendy heels for date night.

4. ***J & Company "Robertson"*** ($175) A narrow-waisted, tailored style for hourglass shapes with enough polish to pair for a blazer sighting.

5. ***Rag & Bone*** ($180) The all-star jean! These slim-cut jeans look great on everyone. Their boot cut is universally flattering, and they sit high on the hips for full tummy and back coverage, so they're muffin top proof.

> *I finally got rid of the "mom" jeans that I've had in my closet for almost ten years! I was so busy with my kids I never took the time to find a new pair of jeans. When you told us where to go and what to try on, I followed your advice. I feel so hot in these new hip jeans! Thanks!*
>
> *Janice*

Short or Tall?

You might be a woman who is really tall or really short. If so, finding jeans is especially frustrating. Are your jeans long or short enough to fit your legs? If not, here are some suggestions for you.

For you tall girls, try stores or brands like Banana Republic, Gap, The Limited, Ellen Tracy, JCPenney, Ann Taylor, Chadwick's, Lands' End, Old Navy, Bill Blass, and Levi's. All of these stores and brands offer jeans in "long" or "tall." For you girls on the short side, try on jeans from Ralph Lauren, JCPenney, Gap, Liz Claiborne, Old Navy, Banana Republic, Not Your Daughter's Jeans, Ann Taylor, Levi's, and Gloria Vanderbilt. All of these stores and brands offer jeans in "petite" or "short."

Plus Size?

For you full-figured gals, it's important to know where to shop to find the best styles for your beautiful body. After doing much research, I have to direct you to the Right Fit brand from Catherine's or the Genius Fit from Lane Bryant. You will find the best jeans for your body type in those stores. They have new technology for denim that won't have your jeans sagging and baggy.

These jeans also come in a variety of lengths — petite, average, and tall. Go to their website or to a store near you to find your perfect pair.

I saw my friend Sharon wearing her new Lane Bryant jeans and she looked like a super model in those things. Girl, she looked hot! Remember, it's not about your size, it's about how you feel about yourself. Sharon is a size 24 – 26 and was the sassiest thing in the room!

Sharon in her Lane Bryant jeans

Jeans are my weakness like shoes are for most women. My favorite pair (I bought four of them) are from Express called Stella. I am 5′1″ and they come in short lengths . . . I love that! They also have some stretch so they are really comfy, and when I bend over you don't see my crack at all . . . y'all gotta love that!

Yvette

Jeans:

Caring for Your Jeans

Bev, a CAbi rep, gave me this great jeans tip: If you love the look of old blue jeans that fade naturally, wash your jeans with like colors in cold water. If you fell in love with your jeans when brand new, you can maintain the consistency of color by simply soaking your jeans in warm water with a cup of salt for about 20–30 minutes, and then wash inside out using a cold water rinse.

Warning: No One Wants to See Your Crack

One of my biggest pet peeves is when a woman bends over or sits down and her rear crack is in plain view. It's gross! I don't want to see it and I'm sure you don't want to see it either. When you try on jeans, make sure you bend over and look in the mirror. Check to see if anything is showing or hanging out. If so, those jeans are not for you.

On the same note, please stay away from too-tight jeans. Form-fitting is definitely flattering, but skintight is not. Remember to be modest when choosing what jeans to wear. Remember, you are representing the beauty of God.

I think we need a little break. It's time to get out of the house. Grab your purse. Grab your keys. Make sure you've got some cash stashed in your wallet or your checkbook, and let's take a road trip … to the nearest mall! It's time to go shopping, girls!

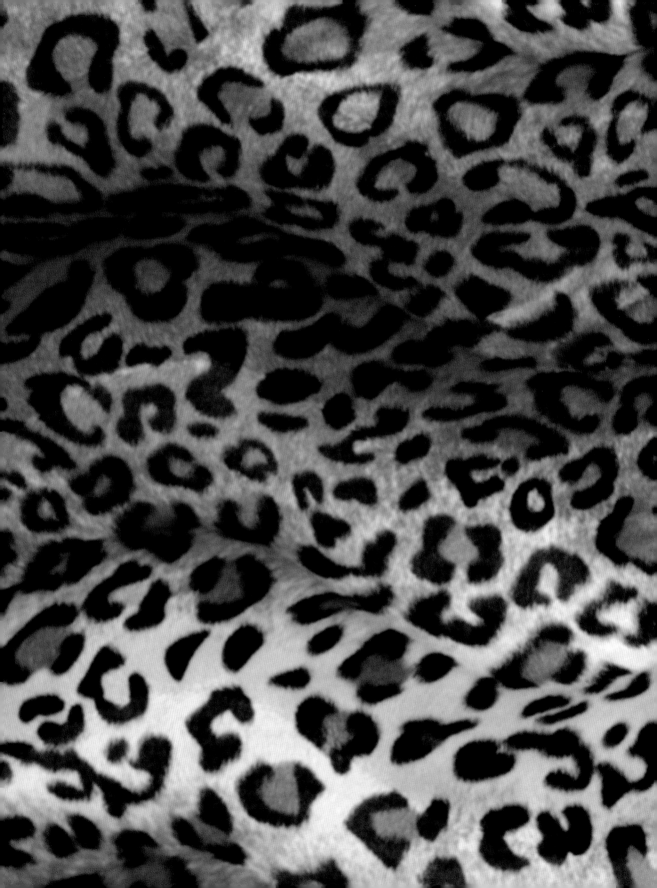

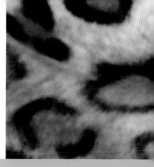

Hit the Mall:
Stop, Drop, and Shop

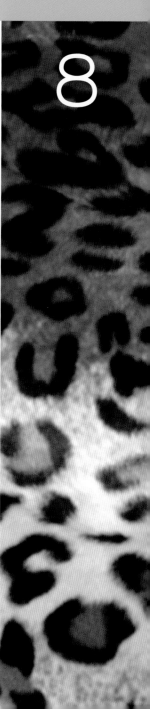

8

From a very young age, women are conditioned to believe that shopping is a hobby. It's meant to be fun and something we're expected to enjoy. It's every teenage girl's passion, and as we get older, many women consider shopping their favorite pastime. So many of us spend numerous afternoons at the mall, meeting our friends for lunch and spending the rest of the day in and out of the various boutiques and shops. For others, however, shopping can be a nightmare. A handful of women dread this activity because they are not sure what to buy, how much to spend, and what they really need.

Whether you love or hate shopping, one thing is certain. We have become a nation of impulse shoppers. We shop anytime, anywhere, and buy whatever strikes our fancy. And boy, finding something on sale is an extra bonus and somehow makes us feel a little less guilty for buying something that, perhaps, we really don't need.

I'm sure you're familiar with the saying, "I've got a closet full of clothes and nothing to wear." Is that something you say on a regular basis? Can you relate at all? I'm sure this statement rings a bell of truth with most of you. Let's be honest. We buy not because we necessarily need, but because we want to feel better about ourselves, because we *have* to have that bag our neighbor has, or because we're bored.

Whatever your reason for impulse shopping, I'm going to ask you to stop doing it starting today. Right now. Some of you, while reading this, might even have gotten bit by the shopping bug just by looking at the title of this chapter and have already been tempted to run out to the mall to buy, buy, buy. No impulse shopping! Just say no!

Don't get me wrong, we are going shopping. That is, of course, the point of this chapter. But I don't mean hobby shopping. It's time to shop on purpose!

Time for a Little Housekeeping

Before you head out, you first have to know what you already own to determine what you will need. If you have your car keys in hand, put them away for a while and spend some time with me in your closet. We're going to do some wardrobe inventory.

Remember, simple is best. The goal of this project is to keep your closets and drawers filled only with those items that you like, are in flattering colors, and fit you just right. Whatever items don't meet this requirement can be donated to a charitable organization, sold to a consignment shop, or given to your friends. The important thing is to get these unwearables out of your house so you're not tempted to wear something that doesn't fit and so you can have a clutter-free closet.

Follow these tips to get this "housekeeping" project started:

The goal of this project is to keep your closets and drawers filled only with those items that you like, are in flattering colors, and fit you just right.

1. If you haven't worn an item in the last year, take it out of your closet. If that item is in a color that you shouldn't be wearing, you don't like it, or you know you'll never fit into it, get rid of it.

2. If you haven't worn an item in the last year because it doesn't fit but you feel confident that you will wear it one day (and it's a great color), take it out of your closet and put it in a storage box with the size written on the outside of the box. If you have too-small clothes of different sizes, put them in separate boxes. If you are currently a size ten, for instance, but have clothes in sizes six, eight, and twelve, organize the clothes in the boxes according to size. Make sure to mark the boxes appropriately and store them in another part of your home, like your attic or another closet.

3. If you have special occasion items that you haven't worn in the last year, find a place for them outside of your regular closet as well.

Hit the Mall:

4. If you have worn an item in the last year, but you're not sure if the color is right for you, get out your color swatches or refer back to chapter 2. Determine what colors work and what won't. Get rid of all the unflattering ones.

5. Try on the clothes you've worn in the last year to assure a proper fit. Do this for those pieces that you're not sure about. Keep or remove the items following the instructions above. If there are pieces you need to get altered, put them in a pile and take them to a tailor when you have some time. At this point, you should now have a pile of clothes that fit you, that you like, and that make you look great. Only these pieces belong in your closet.

6. Organize your closet according to style and color. Hang all pants together and group them by color. Do the same for skirts, dresses, shirts, and so on.

7. Now start making a skeletal inventory list. Take a look at your closet and see if you have more or less of a particular item. For example, do you have more tops or bottoms? Could you use more dresses, skirts, or blouses? Do you have too many pants? Write down the pieces of clothing that you will probably need to buy.

8. Follow the same procedure above for your drawers and other storage areas.

9. Now organize your shoes. Put them in boxes and label them on the outside so you know what kind of shoes are inside. You can also group the summer/spring shoes in one place and do the same with the fall/winter ones.

10. Take a look at your undergarments. By now you know if you need a new bra, but what about your panties? Do you need a shaper? Make a checklist of the undergarments you know you need to purchase.

So What Do I Need?

If you have only a dozen items in your closet, what should they be? I've got your answer right here. Take a look at the following list of essential pieces you should own. If you don't own any of these, they are the first items you should shop for. Start highlighting (go ahead—make the book your own!) the pieces of clothing you'll need to buy so you can add them to the shopping list you have already started.

By the way, you should always keep an ongoing shopping list tucked inside your purse. When you are out and about, running errands, at the mall with a friend having lunch, or on a trip and happen to go into a clothing store, then when you find one of these essential pieces, buy it. This is not impulse shopping; it is a way to shop on purpose.

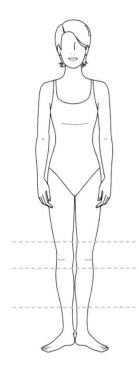

Here is how you can make sure you don't look frumpy

Your hems should hit at an opening or "diamond" on your legs. To determine your best length, stand in front of a full-length mirror, heels together, toes pointing toward 10 o'clock and 2 o'clock. Check to see where your legs touch and where they don't. The places on your legs where your legs don't touch, or rather the "openings" in the legs, are called "diamonds" in your legs. Make sure all lengths, including skirts, dresses, shorts, capris, and cropped pants, end in the center of a diamond.

Hit the Mall:

12 Must-Haves

☐ Jeans in a dark wash to wear with heels or boots

☐ Jeans to wear with flats or casual comfort shoes

☐ A denim jacket in a neutral color. (Mine is brown denim with gold specks from Reba's clothing line. It's sporty, yet functional — and fashionable!)

☐ A white or off-white blouse

☐ A blazer

☐ LBD: Little Black (or Brown) Dress

☐ A cashmere or cotton sweater in a flattering color

☐ A silk or cotton blouse in a print or solid pop color

☐ A V-neck or scoop-neck pullover in your best neutral color. Look for one that has ¾" sleeves.

☐ Khaki, tweed, corduroy, linen, cotton, or wool trousers

☐ Dressy slacks; skinny-ankle or wide-leg pants

☐ A lightweight jacket

If the buttons are the same color as the jacket, consider changing them to a contrasting color like gold or silver to draw attention to the middle of your body. This will make you look slimmer.

Shop for the above pieces based on your clothing personality style. Even though these pieces are classic staples for your wardrobe, you can pull your style into each of these articles. If you're still unsure of your clothing style, then start seeking out these staples in simple styles and add accessories to finish the look. With these dozen basic pieces, you can mix and match to create many different combinations.

The Other Dozen

Building your wardrobe with the twelve pieces I listed on the previous page does not stop there. The following list is what I call "the other dozen." No wardrobe is complete without them. They include:

Don't forget to buy shoulder pads if your hips are wider than your shoulders.

- ☐ A good-fitting bra (although you'll want to eventually have three bras—one to wear, one to rest its elastic to maintain its shape, and one in the wash)
- ☐ A shaper suited to your body type
- ☐ A good selection of panties
- ☐ A fabulous handbag that shows your personality
- ☐ Flats you wear most every day
- ☐ Heels or wedges
- ☐ Riding boots
- ☐ Athletic shoes
- ☐ Hoop earrings in your best metal
- ☐ A ring for your right hand, big or small, your choice
- ☐ A watch that reflects your personality (my friend Heather wears a pink one, I wear a big gold one, and my sister Kathi has one with a polka dot band)
- ☐ Sunglasses

It's almost time to get those car keys out and head to the nearest mall. Are you getting excited yet?

One more thing. I also want to give you a list of particular items you may want to have in your wardrobe for each season. These items are subjective to your needs and desires but may help you out when shopping. By having these pieces in your wardrobe, you won't ever get stuck with having "nothing to wear."

Hit the Mall:

Spring/Summer Basics

- [ ] 2 pairs of shorts
- [ ] 1 pair of capris or cropped pants
- [ ] 2 pairs of lightweight pants in your style preference
- [ ] 4–5 tops in flattering colors and styles
- [ ] 1 lightweight sweater or jacket
- [ ] 2 summer dresses
- [ ] 1 lightweight skirt
- [ ] Comfy casual flats or sandals
- [ ] Trendy sandals in a higher heel or wedge
- [ ] Swimsuit and cover-up
- [ ] 3–4 trendy accessories
- [ ] Summer tote or bag

V-necks or scoop necks create a more visually appealing look and will make you appear slimmer.

Fall/Winter Basics

- [ ] 2–3 pairs of slacks
- [ ] 4–5 tops in flattering colors and styles
- [ ] 2 pullover sweaters
- [ ] 1 blazer
- [ ] 1 party dress
- [ ] 1 longer-length skirt to wear with boots
- [ ] Winter coat in neutral or pop color
- [ ] 2 winter scarves and coordinating gloves
- [ ] 2–3 patterned or solid-colored pairs of tights
- [ ] Flats for everyday wear
- [ ] Dressy boots
- [ ] Classic pumps or slingbacks
- [ ] 3–4 trendy accessories
- [ ] Leather tote or bag

Stop, Drop, and Shop

Shopping According to Your Style

Check out the following shopping guide based on your clothing personality and prices. It will guide you to the brands or retail stores where you'll want to shop to make the most out of your individual style. If you need to, refer back to chapter 3 where the different clothing personalities were explained. These styles will be discussed in the shopping guide so you know exactly what I'm talking about. If you can't find a local retail store with the same name as the brand, browse the web and see which stores carry that brand.

You can pick up whatever essentials you need as I described or purchase some extra pieces to spice up your wardrobe. Don't forget to write down everything you've already highlighted to purchase and bring that list with you so you don't forget a thing!

Keep in mind that the stores I've listed are only a starting point. Before you know it, you'll be able to shop in many different department and specialty stores, consignment stores, thrift stores, and discount stores and be able to spot styles and colors that look great on you and are a good buy.

Guess what? *Now* it's time to hit the mall!

If you're only going to have one handbag, buy a quality one in a color that coordinates with your hair. For example, blondes should choose medium hues of brown and taupe. Dark brunettes should opt for dark brown or black. And of course, pop colors and metallics always work!

Hit the Mall:

Shopping Guide

The Pure Natural woman adores fabrics like cotton, silk, and linen. She wants her wardrobe to reflect the casual lifestyle she lives and the environment and earth she loves so much. She feels best in clothes that are loose, soft, and have an easy, comfortable feel. You will find the Pure Natural woman wearing linen slacks and a blouse to have lunch with a friend and later find her in denim at the ballgame. Her natural style is a breath of fresh air. You won't find many heels in her wardrobe, but may instead find a pair of Rainbows, a comfy linen ballet flat, or low wedges. If you are a laid-back Pure Natural, let me point you in the right direction to stores that reflect your style.

Price Guide Key

$ **Reasonable**

$$ **Mid-Range**

$$$ **Pricey (but worth it!)**

Pure Natural

$	$$	$$$
Buckle	Appleseed's	J. Jill
Christopher and Banks	NorthStyle	Lacoste
JCPenney	LLBean	Soft Surroundings
Old Navy	Land's End	Eileen Fisher

The Classic Modern girl has lots of basics in her wardrobe and loves wearing traditional pieces of clothing and accessories that always have her looking polished and put together. She might add one unusual piece, like a big ring, or splurge on a Kate Spade bag, but she likes to stay understated and chic. A Classic Modern woman always looks sophisticated in a soft, elegant kind of way. She looks likes she's spent a million dollars on her wardrobe yet probably found each piece on sale because she knows exactly what she's looking for and buys it when she finds it. Is this you? If you belong in this category, here is where you can shop to update your wardrobe or find more timeless pieces that suit your taste.

Classic Modern

$	$$	$$$
Dress Barn	Coldwater Creek	Kika
Maurice's	Cato	Banana Republic
Marshall's	The Limited	J. Crew
New York and Company	Talbot's	Michael Kors

Stop, Drop, and Shop

The Creative Original woman has a style all her own. She wears outfits that you would never have even considered putting together, and she looks wonderful. She is the gal who can find a unique jacket that is colorful and bright, and will team it with the artsy skirt she already owns. You'll most likely find her wearing bold patterns like bright florals or zebra prints when she wants to add some splash to her outfits. Other people are always commenting on her one-of-a-kind jewelry and handbags. If you are a Creative Original, these stores and brands are calling out for your unique touch!

Creative Original

$	$$	$$$
Goodwill	Jennifer Lopez	Anthropologie
Ross Dress for Less	Francesca's	Madewell
Ruche	Ruby Road	Boden USA
Vintage Shops	Chico's	Lucky Brand

A Style Fashionista is someone who isn't afraid to wear the latest trends, has no trouble finding pieces that work with items she already has, and loves going big and bold. She can pretty much shop in any store and find something that looks fabulous on her. She stands out in a crowd because she knows what to wear, how to wear it, and how to accessorize it. She is not afraid of the trends and actually makes them look like they've always been in style. If you are a Style Fashionista, here are some brands and stores for you.

Style Fashionista

$	$$	$$$
Forever 21	Loft	Cache
H&M	SteinMart	BCBGMAXAZRIA
TJ Maxx	Express	CAbi
Target	Kohl's	Worth

Hit the Mall:

If you're plus size, tall, or short, take a look at the guides below. These are great places to get fabulous items for harder to find sizes!

Plus Size

Lane Bryant	Dress Barn
Catherine's	Torrid
Avenue	Cato
Ashley Stewart	Maurices

Tall

Long Tall Sally	Chico's
Talllady.com	Gap
Kika	J. Crew
Banana Republic	Old Navy (online)

Petite

Banana Republic	Maurices
Talbots	Kohl's
Old Navy (online)	Land's End
Loft	LLBean

Shopping on purpose is very fulfilling.

As you will soon discover, shopping on purpose is very fulfilling. You will end up with clothes that not only fit and flatter you, but you'll feel really good about how you look. Once you begin dressing in clothes that reflect who you are by wearing styles that tell the world what you are about, you will become confident in your appearance.

I want to encourage you to spend some time looking at different styles, stores, colors, and price points. If you've never loved shopping before, it's highly unlikely you'll love it now, but my guidance should definitely make the experience easier. Follow the steps in this book, one at a time. Once you find a particular store or brand you like, keep shopping there. Find a sales associate who will call you when things go on sale. Find out the name of the people who work there and give them a call every now and then to see if anything new has come in that

Stop, Drop, and Shop

you might like. Give them a list of your sizes and favorite colors and be willing to go in when they call you so you can try things on.

I have one particular store in which I do most of my shopping because they know me and they know what I like. I do the same with the shoe department in this same store. Mick, the sales associate, knows just what kinds of shoes I like so when something new arrives he calls me. The same is true when something goes on sale. We're pretty much BFF's by now!

Shopping becomes so much more enjoyable when you have people who are looking out for you. Finding your style and pieces you like doesn't happen overnight, so make it a plan to spend some time seeking out the clothes you need. There's nothing like experience in the dressing room. Try on, try on, try on!

Now that you're taking the first few steps into becoming more fashionable, I've got to remind you that your clothing choices matter. I don't want you garnering the wrong kind of attention by wearing anything super low-cut or short, so it's time for a lesson in modesty.

Hit the Mall:

Skin *Isn't* In:

Be In without Letting It All Hang Out

9

What Do Our Clothes Say?

Recently I attended a football game with a friend of mine, and her beautiful sixteen-year-old daughter ran into the stands to say hello to us. I have known this family for a long time, and this young woman, who has heard me speak several times, respects my thoughts on fashion and modesty. As Tracy made her way through the bleachers, I noticed she had on the shortest shorts I had ever seen a girl wear. She might as well have been wearing just her underwear. Tracy offered me a cheerful greeting and flashed a million-dollar smile.

It was hard not to notice her barely there clothing. I couldn't *not* say anything. I looked her straight in her eyes and said, "Tracy, why, oh why, are you wearing those short shorts? You are such a positively stunning girl. But guess what? No one is going to notice your amazing face because all they'll be looking at is your bottom half!"

Tracy's response wasn't that positive and she forced a fake smile. I'm sure I made her uncomfortable. She did, however, promise that she would never wear those shorts again. It's a promise I hope she'll keep.

I was sure of one thing. Tracy's self-worth was tied up in the response she was getting from guys who made suggestive comments about her appearance. And no one, not a peer or an adult, had the guts to speak out against it. Not even her parents.

So many young women today are dressing to impress the boys. If you take a stroll through the halls of your local high school, you'll know what I mean. Short skirts, tight shirts, and exposed private parts

175

seem to be the norm. But is the message these girls are sending out the one they really want to be sending?

Recently, I interviewed several high school senior boys (all attractive, athletic, and intelligent) in Florida and asked them about their thoughts on the way girls dress today. Their answers were quite surprising and the consensus the same. All of them said they wished girls understood the message they give off when they dress too sexy.

One teenager commented, "They think they're dressing to get our attention, but they're getting the wrong kind of attention. When we look at them in their barely there clothes, we don't think the thoughts they wish we would think. We actually think less of them. They want us to find them attractive, but we end up thinking things about them that we know they wouldn't want us to think."

Wow! I was blown away. These "hotties" were telling me they would rather their female peers not display their bodies in immodest ways. How come this message isn't one that is being given to our girls or to our women?

Young women today are screaming out to be taught what true beauty is, but nobody is giving them any answers. I get letters from teenagers all the time who tell me about their experiences and challenges being a young woman faced with many societal pressures — maintaining the "perfect" weight, attracting the opposite sex, wearing the right clothes, feeling beautiful, and so on. Take a peek at a letter I received from a nineteen-year-old girl who shared her feelings about her own struggles with body image and her ultimate revelation about true beauty.

Before you leave the house, check yourself in a full-length mirror. Look at all angles. How do you look?

Skin *Isn't* In:

Lately I've been having discussions with my bro's [brothers] in Christ about how hard it is for them when a girl wears revealing clothing because they are wired differently than females. They are very visual creatures, and many young women believe that in order to impress, they need to wear less. But that is so far from the truth if you are trying to attract the right kind of guy.

I struggled with self-image through most of my teen years because I believed the lies satan was feeding me. I couldn't get past the false images in the mirror. I didn't think I was pretty enough and wanted to change everything about my appearance. I felt so out of control that I did what most girls do and blame themselves. When I say "blame" I mean that I chose to turn on myself and tried everything from wearing sexy clothes, diet fads, gym memberships, and soon enough, bulimia. It rocked my world and changed my life.

The funny thing is, I was a Christian and very passionate about Christ, but my actions didn't show it. I was reading my Bible, but I wasn't putting any of it into action. I constantly asked for God's help hoping for some big explosion to make it all better, but it never happened. I never really seemed to care about my worth because all I wanted was beauty. I read all the fashion magazines and watched all the reality shows on TV trying to figure it all out.

One day during my prayer time, it was like a bomb went off when I realized God valued me just as I am. That no matter how few clothes I wore or how skinny I was, I was never going to gain that value from others, nor was I going to value myself. God loved me and valued me, but all I ever wanted was beauty, and I thought the way to finding that was by attracting the opposite sex with the clothes I wore, or lack of them. I finally came to realize that I needed to look to God for my importance, that He wanted to forgive me and I needed to forgive myself for turning to the world and not to Him.

Amen, sister!

It's Not Just Young Girls Either

Young girls and teenagers aren't the only ones who may need some help in the modesty department. On one of my recent layovers in an airport, I stopped by a restaurant to get a Diet Coke. As I ordered my soda at the counter, I noticed a woman in her mid-thirties sitting next to a man who I assumed was her boyfriend. I am not kidding you when I say that I could almost see her nipples because her top was that low cut. And she was not a small-busted woman, either. I then caught a glimpse of the rest of her outfit. Her skirt was very short, and the way she was sitting revealed the tops of her thighs. If I had looked any closer, I might have seen the color of her underwear. No joke.

And then I observed something else. She hardly had on any makeup and she looked absolutely exhausted. Now this might not seem strange to you, but to me it was obvious this woman was struggling with some self-perception issues. Typically, when someone feels good about themselves, even though they may not wear a lot of makeup, they have at least a little on. Even a dab of makeup makes most women feel better. I know it does for me!

My heart ached for this woman. She looked so tired, and her hair was hanging long and straight, hardly looking brushed. There she was showing off her privates for anyone to see. I told my assistant, who was with me at the time, that I was dying to approach her and ask her why she felt the need to dress so provocatively.

Please understand me. I wasn't trying to be mean and I certainly wasn't judging her. In my field, I see this all the time. Women who dress overtly sexy wrestle with their esteem and worth. So for me, I couldn't help but notice that the woman in the airport had, at least on some level, the same struggle. Did she think she was prettier wearing what she was wearing? Did she think her body was her only thing of value? I wanted to talk to her, woman to woman, and share that she was beautiful, makeup or no makeup, but that she was showing the world that she felt her worth came from her body.

What about you? Do you find yourself dressing in clothes that are probably too revealing? Do you make an effort to have some cleav-

We are inundated with images of airbrushed models wearing barely there clothes.

Skin Isn't In:

age showing? Do you gravitate toward super-short skirts? How do you feel about modesty? Do you think your wardrobe reflects that kind of character?

It Starts at Home

See, every woman, teen, and young girl wants to feel beautiful. Tracy, the young woman who wrote me the letter, and the woman in the airport are no different. We are all wired to want to feel attractive, and it's not a bad thing. The problem is that we, as a society, have steered away from what authentic beauty really is. We are told that skin is in. Everywhere we turn — in magazines, TV shows, and billboards — we are inundated with images of airbrushed models wearing barely there clothes. Low-rise and skintight jeans that show our thong underwear are made to look more appealing than a modest sweater set. Our girls have been sold a bill of goods and they've bought it hook, line, and sinker.

I hate to say it, but so have we, their moms. Our girls today dress provocatively because we've been allowing them to dress like this for years. In fact, we're the ones who have chosen their wardrobes for them since they were babies.

Here is what I mean. We put the shortest and cutest skirt on our daughter as soon as she learns to walk because we think she looks adorable. And then our precious girl turns five and we continue to find short, sweet dresses for her to wear and add leotards because it completes the outfit. When she turns ten, we let her wear a mini dress with leggings because all the other girls are wearing that style.

You know what happens next?

At thirteen, our darling daughter enters our living room wearing short shorts and a midriff top. We stare in horror and wonder how in the world she ever got the idea that she could dress like that. When we tell her to put something else on, she responds by rolling her eyes. Then we watch as she heads out the door to hang out with her friends … in, of course, that same outfit.

I know it must hurt a little to read this, but it's a reality. Now here's the best part. You can start right now and teach modesty to your daughter. (And if you need a little help in that department yourself, you can also begin the journey right now.) You can incorporate the fashion guidelines you'll learn about and help your girl not fall into the trap that "skin is in." You can make a difference and help your daughter understand that her inner self is what really matters.

So what can a mom do when a daughter's fashion choices are, well, not based on her mother's good and old-fashioned (but probably outdated and boring) taste? For instance, what if your girl comes home from school all dressed in gothic black? Or when she wants to wear her hair in a ponytail that's dyed pink? Or when she refuses to wear anything other than jeans and a T-shirt to church? Do you ground her until her eighteenth birthday? Take away her cell phone for a week? Make her dress in what you pick out for her until she goes off to college? My advice to you is simple.

Leave it alone!

Yes, I did say that. If it's not sin, leave it alone. What *is* sin when it comes to how we dress? It's wearing clothes that may cause guys to think or act in ways we wouldn't want to be responsible for. Don't get me wrong. Guys are responsible for their own actions, and I'm not letting them off the hook. But because some of them have a serious problem with sex and many are into pornography, we don't want to be a stumbling block on their faith journey.

Now, notice I didn't tell you to back off and not do or say anything. I'd like to share my ideas with you on how you can help your daughter dress and keep peace in your house (and at the mall) all at the same time.

The most important thing to remember is that your daughter probably doesn't think you're very cool and "with it" when it comes to fashion, especially as it concerns *her* idea of fashion. Let's face it, you can be the most stylin' mom there is, but your daughter still doesn't want to dress like you. (And if she does, then I'd say maybe *you* are dressing a little too young for your age!) Having said that, we have to keep in mind that we don't have a say in deciding what's "in" in the fashion

"While clothes may not make the woman, they certainly have a strong effect on her self-confidence — which, I believe, does make the woman."

Mary Kay Ash

Skin *Isn't* In:

world. What we can do, though, is help our girls dress both fashionably and modestly.

What Does Modesty Even Mean?

What comes to mind when you hear the word *modesty*? I'm guessing most of you are probably thinking of words like old-fashioned, boring, puritan, out-of-date, nerdy, and covered up from head to toe. Those are the answers I receive when I ask teens to give me their definition of the word. It's time to clear the air and understand a new meaning for modesty.

Do you know that your outer appearance reflects who you are on the inside? Do you really, really know that? If you answered "yes," then I want you to create a picture in your mind. Imagine a teenage girl wearing a see-through blouse with red bra straps showing; tight, low-rise jeans, baring her midriff; and her thong underwear sticking out of those jeans. Is this image clear? Now think about your immediate impression of her. What kind of girl do you think she is?

Now let's get a second picture in your mind. Picture a teenage girl wearing a low-cut top with her cleavage *slightly* peeking out with a short denim skirt over leggings. She is donning a necklace that has a pendant on the end of it that has slipped inside her top. What's your first impression of her?

Now let's compare the two girls. What did you think of the first girl? If you answered "sleazy" or something similar, then I would agree with you. Now what did you think of the second girl? She was more modest, right? After all, she covered her legs with leggings and her cleavage was only *slightly* peeking out of her top. What's so bad about that? And so what if her pendant has slipped down her shirt? What's the big deal?

The big deal is that guys are visual beings. God created the male brain with some extra special stuff in there that females don't have.

The fact is that boys and men are visually stimulated more than we'll ever be. Let me tell you something: when a boy sees a girl wearing a short skirt with leggings, his mind might not go into overload; but when he sees that necklace creeping down her bosom inside her blouse, he will think, "Gosh, what's down there? I want to see where the necklace goes!" It's how a guy thinks.

You might ask, "But don't we all show a little cleavage every now and then? What's so bad about it?" You might even argue that you are big-busted and you can't help it when you show some of your bosom. I hate to differ with you, but you *can* help it. And you *should* help it. This is where modesty kicks in.

You need to tell your daughter that when she is dressing up cute and sexy to get attention from boys her age, other kinds of guys are looking at her in a way she probably wouldn't want them to. Guys of all ages, from seventeen to seventy ... and that includes guys like her best friend's father! I know it may gross her out to hear that but, believe me, it works. Telling your daughter these things opens her eyes up a bit as to the effect her fashion tastes has on males.

Dressing modestly doesn't mean being old fashioned and dressing puritan-like.

Dressing modestly doesn't mean being old fashioned and dressing puritan-like. What it *does* mean is having an attitude in dressing that reflects a respect for God, our self, and even the opposite sex. Yep, that's it!

I love fashion, especially seeing the trends and crazy styles that come out each season. The cool part about modesty is that I (and you) could wear these popular styles — from short funky skirts to the low-cut tops to the see-through blouses — AND do it modestly. What? Yep, you bet we could.

Modesty is learning how to take each style and make it respectful. Doing this will bring out the fashionista in all of you (and your daughters) by allowing you to be creative with your clothes. So, for example, how could I wear a see-through blouse and still be modest? By wearing it over a cute, colorful tank! (What did you think? That I would wear it alone?) Listen, just because something is in style doesn't make it right for you to wear.

Rules of Modesty

Here's what you need to do. Tell your daughters they can wear anything in the mall, as long as it follows my guidelines. Trust me. They love advice when it comes from a fashion expert and NOT you, their mom. Sorry, but that's how it goes. And hey, if it gets them to understand that how they dress is really about respecting themselves and their guy friends, then we all win!

I'd like to share with you two sets of guidelines for your girl to use when she chooses her outfit or when you two go shopping together. One relates to the inner self (*The 5 Bs of Beauty*), and the other relates specifically to fashion (*The 5 Bs of Style*). Grab a cup of coffee and read on. Make some time later today or tomorrow to read these recommendations with your daughter. It's much easier doing this than complaining about how she dresses and not knowing what to do about it.

Girlfriend, this section doesn't only apply to your daughters. Use this as a guide to make sure *you* are dressing appropriately. You gotta practice what you preach, after all!

Ask yourself, "Would this outfit trip up a guy?"

The 5 Bs of Beauty

RULE #1 **Be yourself.** Dress in what you love and what loves you back.

RULE #2 **Be colorful.** Always wear shades that flatter you and your personality.

RULE #3 **Be satisfied with your body.** Wear the size that fits, not one too small.

RULE #4 **Be beautiful.** Remember you are amazing exactly as you are!

RULE #5 **Be respectful.** Ask yourself, "Would this outfit trip up a guy?"

RULE #1 **_No Bra Straps._** Don't let yours show anywhere, anytime, even if fashion magazines tell you it's the new trend. It's sloppy.

RULE #2 **_No Bust Exposure._** Don't choose clothes that show your cleavage. Make sure your tops aren't too tight at the bust. Wear the correct bra for your size, and never let your nipples show through your clothes.

RULE #3 **_No Bellies._** Treat your tummy as a private part. You wouldn't even think of showing yours to the world, would you? Guys find bellies very sexy, so don't tempt them with yours.

RULE #4 **_No Bottoms._** Don't wear anything with words written on your bottoms. Don't wear your jeans so low your underwear shows. And don't wear your shorts or skirts too short. I recommend keeping them at a length of no more than 2 – 3 inches above the knee. Seriously. No one wants to see up your skirt, except those who shouldn't.

RULE #5 **_No Bubbling._** This is what happens to jeans when they are too tight. Check yours by looking at the back of your thighs. If you have ridges and wrinkling in that area, this means your pants are too tight. Try a different style or size, or both. (See page 155.)

Skin _Isn't_ In:

Stop the Shopping Wars

Many girls have a penchant for pushing the limits to accentuate and expose their changing bodies. They watch their friends dress suggestively and they want to dress that way too. What they don't understand is that when they choose clothing to highlight their private areas, they not only disrespect others but they disrespect themselves. You can help break this pattern.

Make shopping a fun experience, even if it hasn't been in the past.

One thing you can do is to make shopping a fun experience, even if it hasn't been in the past. You must be very proactive in planning your shopping outing. To do this, shop alone with your teen daughter. Leave siblings and friends at home. Tell her you want to find out what is in fashion for girls her age, and that you're going to be open to what she picks out. Ask her to show you what she likes and promise not to comment about her selections (unless it's positive). This might be hard, but you can do it!

Spend an hour or so looking at her choices, then tell her it's time for a break and go to a coffee shop. If she's like most teen girls, she loves coffee, so she'll be all over this idea. Then spend some time talking about modesty. Ask her what she thinks it means and help her to understand that it's an attitude of respecting God, herself, and her guy friends. Show her the *5 Bs of Beauty and Style* and then tell her you are going to go back to the store to buy her an outfit. As long as it covers these guidelines and is within your budget (tell her the budget ahead of time), she can take it home. Now watch her have some fun!

Your daughter may not come home with the outfit you would have chosen (please, please, please, let her pick it and try to keep quiet), but she will come home with an outfit that will be respectful. And another thing, just because you think that being respectful to God means wearing a dress in church, it may not be what God thinks. I think He'd prefer you getting along on Sunday morning, and not arguing. Give your daughter the space to make her fashion choices, whatever that might be, as long as they are guided by these basic principles of modesty. I can guarantee that your shopping experiences will be full of so much joy and pleasure from now on.

So Skin Isn't In?

Nope, it's not. Never. Ever. But I think you've figured that out by now. So should you teach your girls to cover up from head to toe? Absolutely not! Girls need to understand that what they wear on the outside tells the world who they are on the *inside*.

Friend, don't just use this chapter as a guide to teach your daughter modesty. Use it as a guide for yourself as well. Whatever your age, whether you have children or not, this message is relevant to you. After all, you are a role model for someone. I know some of you are older and have a rocking body that you want to show off. Remember, it doesn't mean you need to squeeze into super short shorts or a too-tight shirt. Let your inner beauty shine, not your outer parts.

As Christians, we've been called to a higher standard. Teach your daughter that calling, and act as a role model for her in your own wardrobe choices. Before you walk out the door, take a look in a full-length mirror and ask yourself, "If I were to run into 'me' today, who would I say I am based on what I'm wearing?" Remind your daughters to ask themselves this same question and you won't have to fight the clothing wars much longer.

A Word from Shari

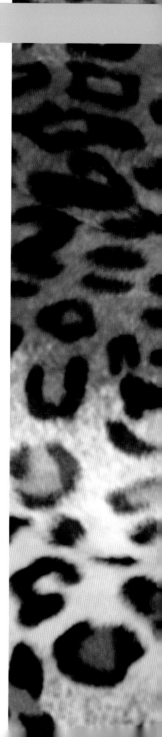

I FELT SO HONORED WHEN I READ THE FOLLOWING LETTER. I WAS deeply encouraged to hear how much this woman had learned, and I hope you share some of her same thoughts.

> *Shari, I just wanted to tell you that the information and the advice you gave to me at our MOPS meeting was so helpful and has since stuck with me! Though I tend to be a little forgetful, I have not forgotten what you taught me about fashion and style. You taught me about my body shape; appropriate lengths on skirts, dresses, and cropped pants; how to wear the right size and amount of accessories; and what colors to wear and not to wear. Even though I have little time to shop for myself, I know that when I purchase something, it will look great and feel right (no matter what the size — I can cut the tag out!) I learned that God did not make a mistake with me, and that I am beautiful just the way I am!*
>
> *Dawn*

"For we are God's masterpiece. He has created us anew in Christ Jesus, so we can do the good things he planned for us long ago" (Eph. 2:10 NLT).

Do you feel made new? Do you know you are a masterpiece specifically created by God? While our time together is almost done, I pray this is just the beginning for you. We have taken this ride of personal style and fashion together, and I hope you have learned valuable information that will make you sparkle inside and out with God-given confidence. I have been (and will continue to be) your cheerleader along this new adventure, because I know that God ordained this project, and I believe He wants me to help you see yourself in a fresh way, a beautiful way.

All the colors, styles, haircuts, and tips aside, I want you to know and always remember one thing: You are a uniquely created woman and God did NOT make a mistake with your body. You have been given the exact features and shape that you are supposed to have, the perfect color eyes for you, and the hair color that naturally suits you best. You are a masterpiece, indeed. And guess what else? The God of the universe thinks you are amazing!

I hope this book has given you permission to take care of yourself. It is OKAY to spend time on your outer appearance and look your best. And I have equipped you with the tools, guides, and know-how so you can do this feeling empowered. You now know how to look fabulous!

I would be remiss if I let you finish reading this book without addressing your inside. Girlfriend, being beautiful starts with knowing who God is. You see, I didn't come to know who God really is until I was almost thirty years old. I didn't grow up in a church where a personal relationship with Jesus was stressed. Oh yes, we learned about God and who Jesus was, but it was very ritualistic. I didn't own a personal Bible and honestly never even held one up close until a woman named Mari invited me to go to a Bible study. I didn't want to go, but she persisted and refused to accept my excuses. So, almost three months later, I finally relented. To tell you the truth, the only reason I

It is OKAY to spend time on your outer appearance and look your best.

Help Me, Jesus! I Have Nothing to Wear!

went was to get her off my back. Little did I know how that morning would change the course of my life.

It was at that Bible study where I learned that I could have a personal, real, one-on-one relationship with God through His son, Jesus. I came to know who Jesus was in the living room of a woman named DeAnn, because another woman named Mari kept asking me to go. DeAnn explained coming to know God in a way I had never heard before. No one had ever told me that God wanted to be involved in my life and even had a plan, a specific direction, for my future. "For I know the plans I have for you, plans to prosper you and not to harm you, plans to give you hope and a future" (Jer. 29:11).

I didn't know God was loving and invested in my life. I thought God was part of the impersonal and cold religion I had known as long as I could remember. I didn't know there was real life, transformation, and a depth to living a life for God. You might know what I'm talking about. As a matter of fact, you might be in the same shoes I was in, when Mari first invited me to that Bible study. Maybe you've never been told about this kind of God either. Maybe you read this book, saw some references to God and Bible verses, and thought, "Oh, how nice, Shari must be religious, but that is certainly not for me."

Here's the thing. I'm not religious. And I don't want you to be religious either. I want you to be in *relationship*. In relationship with a God who loves you more than you can ever imagine. Some of my favorite verses in the Bible actually come right *after* the verse I just told you about: "Then you will call upon me and come and pray to me, and I will listen to you. You will seek me and find me when you seek me with all your heart. I will be found by you," declares the Lord, "and will bring you back from captivity" (Jer. 29:12 – 14).

Think about your own life. Are you in captivity, waiting to be led back to life? I know I was. But I didn't even know it at the time. I thought my life was perfectly fine and dandy. Who cares that I was on my second marriage, was living with way too much guilt for past actions, that I wasn't the friend I wished I had been to so many, and was always looking to others for approval? Sure, I could have kept living that way, attending a church where ritual was more important than relationship, but you know what would have happened? I never would have known the life God had planned for me because I would have kept living it the way I, Shari, had planned. I probably wouldn't even have written this book.

Now, my life before God wasn't all that bad. I lived in a nice house, had a good job, drove a great car, and had wonderful friends. I could have continued living that way and never have known the fullness that was available to me through a life in Christ. But you see, Mari didn't give up on me. I believe with all my heart that God entrusted her with the job of inviting me to that Bible study. The women in that fabulous group mentored me, taught me, loved on me, and showed me what real beauty was. Real Beauty, my friend, is God.

Life wasn't perfect after I invited God into my heart. I had so much learning to do and many more mistakes to make. In fact, for a time I turned away from God and tried to live Shari's way again. But it just didn't work. I eventually turned back to God and committed myself to walking with Him. I made the decision to live life His way, not mine.

Maybe you've been a Christian for a long time but you've tried to do things your way. It's never too late to turn back to God and ask Him to walk before you. All you have to do is ask Him to come into your life and lead you. And He will.

And now, my new friend, it's time to go forth knowing that you are okay just the way you are. You can step out of this book and be made anew, on the outside AND the inside. There are many books and resources available on being beautiful on the inside, so I'd encourage you to pick one up and go deeper.

As I send you off, I pray you see yourself beautiful. I pray you have looked at yourself in a new way and have seen something delightful. I encourage you to walk forward with newfound confidence in how to dress your outer appearance. Follow the guidelines I've detailed for you throughout this book and know that you CAN do this! Being in style and dressing to look your best is not hard. Stop comparing yourself to the models you see in the magazines or the alpha mother you see at

It's time to go forth knowing that you are okay just the way you are.

Help Me, Jesus! I Have Nothing to Wear!

church or your children's school. Stop being so hard on yourself and love on yourself the way God loves on you.

Accepting myself in God's eyes was tough for me. One of my biggest struggles was seeking the approval of others. I wanted to be beautiful in the eyes of everyone else (though I didn't know how to be beautiful for me). I know this is something that many women deal with. We seek comfort and confidence in shopping, plastic surgery, our kids, dieting, or wearing sexy clothes. But what we need to do is stop relying on stuff and others to feel good or beautiful or put-together or perfect. Only Jesus Christ can give us our true identity. It's only found in Him.

I hope you will email me, visit my blog or join us at our *Fashion Meets Faith* Facebook community, and let me know how you are doing. I'd love to see some pictures of you too!

And so for now, I send you off the same way we started.

Go stand in front of a mirror. Take a deep breath. Smile, look straight ahead, and realize that … *You* are the woman in that mirror. *You* are a Christian. *You* have permission to take care of your outer appearance. And no more will you yell, "Help me, Jesus! I have nothing to wear!"

So, how do you look?

Gorgeous, I say.

Absolutely gorgeous.

Acknowledgments

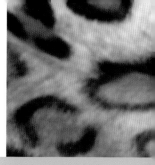

I'M GLAD YOU PAUSED TO READ THIS PAGE, BECAUSE WITHOUT THE help and support of these amazing people, this book would never be what it is and I'm deeply appreciative for them.

To Sandy Vander Zicht: You are not only my editor but you are my friend. I can't imagine working with anyone else. Thank you for pushing for this book and always remember that when in doubt, wear cat socks.

Beth Shagene: Talented, artistic and altogether a creative rock star for designing the best book interior ever! Moah!

Carly Crookston: I am so grateful for your attention to detail and your sweet, sincere, calm spirit. You made the editorial process seem easy. I appreciate you more than you know.

Sarah Johnson: Working behind the scenes, it's because of YOU that the book looks so good! Thank you for your diligent, hard work. I am so very grateful!

Londa Alderink: Thank you for your resourceful, inspired ideas to make sure the masses knew about this book. I love working with you!

To Marybeth Whalen, Lisa Shea, and Lisa Whittle: You make being in ministry fun. Thank you for always having my back and promising to slap me down if I ever get too big for my britches.

To Patti Hedge, Sharon Haddad, Tanya McCorkle, and Susan Hughes: Your friendship is a breath of fresh air and I love our monthly outings. Can we have another one soon?

To Renee Harris, Darya Suddreth, Libby Williams, Kim Shaw, Kathie Parson, Mary Brandes, Gabi Goni, and Sharon Glasgow: You each bring something special to my life. Thank you for understanding that friendship doesn't always mean being in the same location, otherwise I'd have no friends!

To Susan Seay, Donna Roland, Tabitha Dumas, and Laura Gutnecht: You soooo make me look good! My ministry would not be what it is without each of you. I am honored you do what you do for me.

To Esther Fedorkevich: You are always in my corner and I so love that about you.

To Christy Bass: You are a rock star in my book. Thank you for your beautiful photography and for leading us each and every Monday morning at Moms In Prayer.

To my Sunday School Class at Northside Baptist Church in Charlotte, NC: You ladies rock! I love spending Sunday mornings with you.

To my husband, Dave: You are exactly who I need. You are always behind the scenes but I couldn't do what I do without your love and support. You are amazing.

To my son, Luke: I am so proud of you and the fact that you always put Jesus first.

To my Steppies: When I married your dad, I married you. I love you dearly.

To my Dad, Sam Morrison: Though you're over 80, you're still inventing and I so love that about you!

To Wendi Davis and Kathi Carroll: You are the best sisters in the world … I'm so glad we are close.

To my blog readers, Facebook friends, and Twitter followers: You are all amazing people and you encourage me every day.

And to Jesus: To You, I owe it all.

Help Me, Jesus! I Have Nothing to Wear!

Special Acknowledgment and Thanks to:

Alysa Garrick Photography

LEAD PHOTOGRAPHER: **Alysa Garrick**

Belk

Charlotte, NC

WEBSITE: www.Belk.com (extra thanks to Michele Dickey)

Christy Bass Photography

Christy Bass, Charlotte, NC

Denim Affair

Charlotte, NC

WEBSITE: www.denimaffaironline.com

Dillard's

Charlotte, NC

> *Thank you* to my beautiful blog readers whose comments are used throughout this book.

Hair Designer

Cindy Russell, Hair Achitecture and Design, Charlotte, NC

In His Image Photography by Julie

LEAD PHOTOGRAPHER: **Julie Staley,** Waxhaw, NC

ASSISTANT PHOTOGRAPHER: **Laura Stikeleather,** Waxhaw, NC

WEBSITE: InHisImageByJulie.com

Kika

Los Angeles, CA

LensCrafters

Makeup Artist

Kenna Ehman, Modern Salon and Spa, Aveda, Charlotte, NC

Mary Kay Cosmetics

MAKEUP ARTIST: **Jordan Helou Eicher,** Huntersville, NC
WEBSITE: marykay.com/jordanhelou
MAKEUP ARTIST: **Danai Garay,** Charlotte, NC
WEBSITE: marykay.com/danaigaray

Southern Girl Photgraphy

LEAD PHOTOGRAPHER: **Whitney Tucker**

Stylists

LEAD STYLIST: **Patti Curlee**
ASSISTANT STYLIST: **Kimberly Zubke**
JUNIOR STYLIST: **Mattie McGinnis**

Models

Erica Baxter-Smith	Lori Kempers	Erika Reiner
Jazmin Brownaft	Yvette Lavender-Smith	Elizabeth Reiner
Kristi Butler	Sandra Leach	Donna Roland
Stephanie DiMora	Kaitlin Lewis	Susan Russell
Sandra Fish	Diane Lipiec-Fauver	Kathy Silva
Lauren Frye	Tammi Marohn	Tara Tomlinson
Michelle Gray	Jill Marquis	Lisa Whittle
Andrea Haddad	Myra Mason	Rashele Yarborough
Sharon Haddad	Dawn Massey	Samantha Yoxtheimer
Renee Harris	Abbe Massuccy	Jenny Zedalis
Christy Horwitz	Brittney Overstreet	Jill Zimmerman
Michelle Hyatt	Rebekah Phillips	
Hannah Jones	Stacey Price	

Resource List

Following is a list of websites for products mentioned in this book. These products are recommendations from personal use and from other's experiences, but feel free to try other things to see what works for you. The products listed throughout this book were available at the time of printing; however product lines often change and we cannot guarantee their availability at all times. If you have trouble finding a product mentioned in this book, please email Shari@FashionMeets Faith.com.

Ann Taylor
Anthropologie
Albert Makali
Antonio Melani
Ashley Stewart
Anne Klein
Avon
Assets by Sara Blakely
Aveeno
Avenue

Banana Republic
Bill Blass
Brooks Brothers
Bali

B. Tempt'd
Buckle, The

CAbi
Chadwick's
Catherine's
Coldwater Creek
Chico's
Color Swatch Shopping Guide
Color E-nalysis
Citizens of Humanity
Clinique
Carlisle Collection
Charlotte Russe
CJ Banks

Resource List *cont.*

Coach
Color Me Beautiful
Chanel
Cabernet
Cetaphyl
Curél
Carol Wior

Doncaster
Dillard's
DKNY
Deva Curl
Delta Burke
Dress Barn
Diane von
    Furstenberg

Eddie Bauer
Ellen Tracy
Elizabeth Arden
Express
Essential Bodywear
Estée Lauder
Eileen Fisher

Fashion Bug
Forever 21
Fantasizer

Gloria Vanderbilt
Gilligan & O'Malley

Gel Petals
Gap

H&M
Hanes
How to Have Style
    by Issac Mizrahi

In His Image
    Photography
IsABelt
Inches Away

JCPenney
J. Jill
Joe's Jeans
Jones New York
J.Crew
Jasmine Ginger
Jockey

Kmart
Kate Spade
Kohl's
Karen Kane
Kasper

Lands' End
Levi's
Lane Bryant
Liz Claiborne
Louis Vuitton

Lee
Limited, The
Longitude
Lancôme
Lucy Brand

Michael Kors
Maidenform
Mary Kay Cosmetics
Macy's
Miraclesuit
Miratex
Magicsuit

Nordstrom
Not Your Daughter's
    Jeans
Nurture
New York and
    Company
Nieman Marcus
Neutrogena

Old Navy
Origins
Olay

Pixi
Premier Designs

Ralph Lauren
Reba

Rainbow
Ross Dress for Less
Ruby Road
Riders by Lee
Revlon

Saks Fifth Avenue
Simply Vera
    by Vera Wang
SteinMart
ShariBraendel.com
Starbucks
Spanx
Sarah Blakely
Smashbox
Seven7

Target
Talbots
T.J. Maxx
Talllady.com
Tommy Hilfiger

Vanity Fair

Walmart
Willie Smith
White House Black
    Market
Wacoal

Help Me, Jesus! I Have Nothing to Wear!

Notes and Image Credits

Notes

1. *NIV Study Bible* (Grand Rapids: Zondervan, 2008), p. 1930.

2. Isaac Mizrahi, *How to Have Style* (New York: Gotham, 2008).

Image Credits

Alysa Garrick Photography: 60

Belk: 33, 40, 42, 43, 77, 78, 80

Christy Bass Photography: 57 (2), 58 (4), 59 (3), 60 (2), 61 (2), 62 (2), 130 (3), 131 (3)

Erica Carryl of Vine & Branch Photography, CT: 60

In His Image Photography by Julie Staley: 31, 34, 35, 37, 39, 41, 71, 87 (2), 91 (2), 92 (5), 94 (4), 105, 106, 107, 108 (2), 109, 121 (3), 122 (3), 123 (3), 124 (3), 128 (2), 146 (3), 147 (2), 151 (2), 152, 153, 155, 160

Illustrations by Monika Roe: 28 (2), 29 (2), 107, 108 (2), 109, 119, 166

iStockphoto®: leopard print: 17, 50, 55, 63, 75, 87, 98, 110, 120, 129, 149, 157, 160, 177

denim background: 150, 151, 152, 153

others: 14, 25, 38, 51, 66, 73, 74, 75, 82, 86, 88, 89, 100, 103, 110, 111 (2), 116, 117, 125, 126, 127, 133, 134, 136, 138, 139, 140, 142, 143, 148, 149, 165, 167, 168, 169, 170, 174, 179, 184

Kika: 34, 40, 44, 45, 46, 61 (2), 79

shutterstock®: 32, 36 (2), 42, 76, 81, 168, 169 (2), 181, 184 (3), 185, 191

Southern Girl Photography: 57